Hitting Hard

MICHELANGELO SIGNORILE

CARROLL & GRAF PUBLISHERS

NEW YORK

HITTING HARD

Carroll & Graf Publishers
An Imprint of Avalon Publishing Group Inc.
245 West 17th Street
New York, NY 10011

AVALON
publishing group incorporated

Library of Congress Cataloging-in-Publication Data is available.

ISBN: 0-7867-1619-3

Book design by Jamie McNeely
Printed in the United States of America
Distributed by Publishers Group West

To Mary Cheney, Arthur Finkelstein and the rest of the gang.
May they each find a conscience.

CONTENTS

FOREWORD

It's fitting to begin this collection in the year 1996, with the piece "Outing's Triumphant Return." It was the year when the issue of same-sex marriage, for the first time, became a tool for the national Republican Party. Conservative politicians saw how they could use the issue as a cudgel against Democrats, many of whom until this day haven't figured out how—nor have developed the backbone—to stand up and fight back.

For gay activists, the issue of "outing" once again catapulted to the forefront in 1996, just as it has again today, directed at those members of Congress who vote to define marriage to exclude gays. It's clear looking back now that the period midway through Bill Clinton's presidency was the beginning of a new era—for gay bashing by Christian conservatives as well as for the closet.

Much of the late 1990s and the early part of the twenty-first century, for me, was about seeing how the closet played out—sometimes violently—while traveling the United States and the world. Many of the pieces here are my reports and reflections on those travels, from the heart of Mormon Country to the Deep South, and from the far reaches of New Zealand to the southern tip of Italy. I also looked at the many ways we all relate to our families, no matter where we live. "Homo for the Holidays," written in 1996 about my relationship with my own family, received an enormous response after it was published.

Another piece here that garnered an extraordinary amount of feedback was "The Truck Stops Here," about my travels on the road with two gay truckers. Like some of the other pieces included here—"Transgendered Nation" and "Queer in a Million" both come to mind—I hope that the response reflected some readers' realization of the amazing diversity among us, while others perhaps saw themselves reflected in the pieces after having often felt invisible.

While queer visibility is certainly on display here, this collection is about more than gay politics and culture. It charts the progression of this country from the Clinton years into the current Bush era. It reflects on the September 11 attacks and their aftermath, as well as the Bush administration's exploitation of the war on terrorism. It looks at the war in Iraq and the lies that led up to it. And it covers the dangerous shifts that have occurred in American politics and culture, as the Christian right has been mainstreamed into the Republican Party and into our government. These ten years will likely be looked back upon as among the most pivotal periods in American history.

May 2005

OUTING'S TRIUMPHANT RETURN

YES, IT WAS THE year of the antigay Defense of Marriage Act (DOMA) and endless media debates about how and whether to recognize gay and lesbian unions, but the most remarkable gay marriage that happened in 1996 was the one between many gay conservatives and gay progressives over the issue of questioning public figures' sexual orientation. Who would have thought that it would take an issue as conservative as the celebration of monogamy and stability to bring back an issue as explosive and disruptive as outing?

DOMA did it. The anger unleashed by that piece of legislation, which banned federal recognition of same-sex marriage and allowed states to do the same, radicalized and reenergized many lesbian and gay Americans. Many of us were shocked that legislators whom we knew or thought to be closeted gay men and lesbians could vote for this particularly nasty, antigay bill. On a personal level (and not always in my role as a journalist), I angrily confronted more than one closeted politician at public events, and also sent out reports online. Indeed, in the midst of the debate over DOMA this summer, the Internet became ablaze with outings, as many of the staid and often conservative gay marriage advocates teamed up with notorious queer activists like Michael Petrelis to attempt a major cleaning of Washington's closets. For perhaps the first time, information about American legislators' sexuality raced around the globe, popping up on home pages, in e-mail messages, on bulletin boards, in newsgroups, on Web sites, in chat rooms. The mainstream and more traditional media became almost superfluous. After all, when you've got the World Wide Web, who needs the *New York Times*?

Not all of the tales were well documented, of course, and some were mere speculation based on apocryphal anecdotes. Regardless, in light of the passage of DOMA, many gay men and lesbians felt it was well within their rights to speculate about which senators and members of Congress might be queer. Certainly wondering whether someone might be gay or lesbian was not in and of itself a bad thing, they reasoned. Eventually, many of the online outings spilled over onto gay radio broadcasts and gay cable TV shows, into the gay and alternative print media, and then often into the mainstream. Several members of the House and Senate, even if they denied assertions that they were lesbian or gay, or if they refused to answer the question at all, were this year asked point-blank by reporters about their sexual orientation.

Such questioning would have been unthinkable in years past.

Indeed, what was perhaps most remarkable about all of this was how unremarkable it all was. Several of the Internet-driven outings made it into the mainstream with little of the moral outrage we'd come to expect from the national media on the issue. Though Representative Mark Foley of Florida, a pro-DOMA Republican, would neither confirm nor deny reports in the gay press about his sexual orientation, for example, those reports eventually surfaced in the *St. Petersburg Times* and other newspapers, with barely a whimper from the privacy purists in the national press.

Even the most highly publicized outing this year was received practically with open arms: Congressman Jim Kolbe, a pro-DOMA Arizona Republican at the center of the Internet outing campaign, eventually became exasperated by the pressure and, knowing that the *Advocate* was about to out him, decided to come out on his own. But while the local paper in his home state, the *Arizona Republic,* flew into a temper tantrum and attacked the outers, most of the national media and the more prominent urban dailies failed to produce the editorial reprimands or op-ed pieces we've come to expect, or even to offer up the usual articles focusing on the ethics of outing. In fact, while the *New York Times* and other papers included in their pieces about Kolbe's forced coming out an obligatory quote or two from gay people opposed to outing (mostly Log Cabin Republicans who'd been friendly with Kolbe while he was closeted), the *Washington Post* didn't bother to quote anyone who was against outing or even to refer to outing as controversial. In the nation's capital, it appeared, outing had become an accepted fact of American politics.

It seems like a lifetime ago, but it's been a mere six years since outing first blew onto the American political and cultural landscape. It was in January 1990 that *Time* magazine, never previously so concerned about the civil liberties of homosexuals, suddenly decided there was a new and vicious threat to gay individuals lurking in the gay press itself. Quickly, they had to rout out the perpetrators and label this menace. Thus the term "outing" was born.

From the beginning, I was at the center of the storm, having written columns in the now-defunct *OutWeek* magazine at the time exposing the homosexuality of various closeted public figures in New York and Hollywood who were in bed (sometimes literally) with the very homophobes who were beating us down. I believed, as I still do, that this was simply good and proper reportage, no different from what the rest of the media were doing with regard to reporting on straight public figures who preach one way and practice another. Certainly, it should not have its own special name, particularly one with such a negative connotation. My editor at *OutWeek,* Gabriel Rotello, attempted to rename this phenomenon "equalizing," stressing that we were simply equalizing the discussion in the media of homosexuality and heterosexuality. But others begged to differ. Practically every major news organization in the country, not to mention various prominent straight and gay individuals, condemned us for what they saw as reckless journalism.

The writer Fran Lebowitz, usually known for her subtly sardonic quips rather than bombastic overstatements, voiced what was then a standard reaction to outing, both inside and outside the gay community: "It's damaging, it's immoral, it's McCarthyism, it's terrorism, it's cannibalism, it's beneath contempt. . . . To me this is a bunch of Jews lining up other Jews to go to the concentration camps."

Lebowitz's statement came shortly after I'd written a cover story in *OutWeek* in March 1990 about the recently deceased multimillionaire (and New York party chum of Lebowitz's) Malcolm

Forbes, revealing that he was gay. Somehow, reporting this simple fact, even though it was true and even though the man was now dead, was seen as the most grotesque and slanderous thing one could do in 1990. The usually news-starved American press corps was completely at a loss as to how to proceed on this one.

In typical tabloid tradition, New York's *Daily News* had planned to run the story on its front page (having been given an advance copy) as soon as *OutWeek* hit the stands. But the paper spiked it at the last minute, saying it was too "sensational"; instead, the *News* ran with a story about Donald and Ivana Trump's divorce, all about how Mr. Trump's mistress, Marla Maples, had hid in Trump Tower.

Believe it or not, it took a period of months for references to the Forbes story to surface in papers around the country, and that was mostly in articles about the terrible new thing called "outing." The *New York Times* was among the last papers to cover the outing-as-the-new-fascism story; in its piece, however, unlike many of the other papers, the *Times* refused to name Forbes, saying only that "a recently deceased businessman" had been outed.

Shift to 1996: In a lengthy front-page, above-the-fold story about Republican presidential primary candidate Steve Forbes in February headlined, "In Political Quest, Forbes Runs in Shadow of Father," the *New York Times* not only told its readers about "the first published reports in the gay press of his father's homosexuality," but went on to question Mr. Forbes about the issue and to enlighten us about the fact that "in the last five years of his life, Malcolm Forbes became increasingly indiscreet, and he was seen regularly roaring up on his motorcycle in tight black leather to Manhattan nightclubs and, according to current and former workers at *Forbes* [magazine], pursuing some of his young male employees."

The world has changed.

And clearly the change did not occur just because many gay people have suddenly come to see outing those who voted against them as an essential political strategy. The DOMA outings were, in fact, capitalizing on a process that had been taking place for several years within the American media. As the *Times*'s Forbes turnaround underscores, journalistic outing never really went away and only progressed as time went on. Its perimeters are still hazy and unstable, changing as often as the public's feelings about homosexuality itself change, and there no hard-and-fast rules. The simple fact is that more and more journalists are coming to realize that there are times when a public figure's undisclosed homosexuality is relevant and proper to report on or to speculate about, regardless of whether that person is directly engaging in antigay behavior or not.

The highly publicized outing of Assistant Secretary of Defense Pete Williams in 1991, a story I wrote for the *Advocate,* perhaps gave much of the media the first clear-cut example of the so-called hypocrisy argument for outing: Williams was a spokesperson for the Pentagon, an institution that had a particularly vicious policy against allowing gay men and lesbians to serve in the armed forces, regularly conducting witch-hunts to purge gay service members. But while most of the press picked up the story, they were baffled as to how to treat it: Some news organizations ran the story prominently and named Williams; others buried it, saying only that "a Pentagon official" had been outed.

Fast-forward four years.

By the time *Rolling Stone* publisher Jann Wenner left his wife in 1994 for former Calvin Klein employee Matt Nye, the idea of relevancy—as distinct from hypocrisy—had become established: The *Wall Street Journal* published a front-page piece on

Wenner's divorce and the effect it would have on his business empire (his wife was his business partner), clearly seeing the relevance of reporting the fact that Wenner left his wife for a man. Had Wenner left his wife for a woman, the paper reasoned, it would have reported that and other facts about her. The rest of the media picked up the Wenner story quickly. And the *Washington Post,* as if the editors there had come up with the idea on their own, decided all of this needed a new name: the "equalization" of homosexuality and heterosexuality.

Though we may be getting there, however, "equalization" is not yet quite, well, as equal as many of us would like it to be. While outing is now within the realm of popular journalism, much of the media still duck for cover when it comes to the lives of public figures who are gay or lesbian, not quite knowing how to proceed, often fearful of coming under attack if they move too quickly. Holding all the cards (though the Internet is beginning to usurp their power), the mainstream media still make arbitrary decisions about who to out and who not to out. For example, when Republican political strategist Arthur Finkelstein—a man who worked for such illustrious homophobes as Republican senators Jesse Helms, Lauch Faircloth, and Don Nickles—was revealed by *Boston* magazine in October to be gay and living with another man and their two adopted children in a posh corner of Massachusetts, much of the media seemed to walk on eggshells. The story swirled around a bit, surfacing in the *Village Voice,* getting a mention in *Newsweek,* a blurb in the *New York Post,* and a relatively short segment on CNN's *Headline News.*

Finkelstein clearly didn't want this information about his life plastered across the media (as it could—and probably did—cost him clients like Mr. Helms); he refused to speak on the record with the *Boston* reporter about the topic and later issued a statement saying he was "disappointed" with the story: "I keep my private life separate from my business life." But because Finkelstein, in the context of his disapproval of the revelations, noted that his "family" knew he was gay, the story suddenly seemed okay for the *New York Times* to get its hands dirty over. The eagle-eyed columnist Frank Rich wrote a stinging column about Finkelstein, making sure to note that Finkelstein was out to his family. But mentioning this fact seemed to be splitting hairs: For all practical purposes, the *Times* was also outing Finkelstein, a private man who, by his own refusal to speak on the record about his sexuality with the *Boston* magazine reporter (or with the *Times* itself), did not want this information made public. The *Times* could say that it wasn't an outing, but there are many other public figures whose homosexuality is just as relevant as Finkelstein's and who have for years been just as out to their families, and even to their local communities (Congressman Kolbe and many other, still-closeted members of Congress come to mind). But the *Times,* and many other media organizations, remain fearful of discussing these people's sexuality.

Part of the reason is that outing—the word itself—is something no one wants to be associated with (and despite even the *Washington Post*'s best efforts, equalizing is not catching on). Just like the words "feminist" and "liberal," the word "outing" has been demonized, even though most people probably believe its basic tenets or support it to some extent. When the producers of *Ellen* this year decided to toy with the idea of making the lead character come out as a lesbian, *Time* magazine let us know that *Ellen* star Ellen DeGeneres's own sexual orientation "is a topic of much speculation." Certainly, it was relevant for *Time* to discuss the issue, as did much of the media, including syndicated *Boston Globe* columnist and veteran feminist Ellen Goodman. Astute about the taint of the O word, Goodman in fact noted that "when *New York* magazine reported spotting [DeGeneres] at a Manhattan bar kissing a woman, it started a controversy about the difference between 'outing' and celebrity reporting." (Well, that's exactly the point, Ms. Goodman: There is no difference.) And *Time*'s editors, too, would be loath to admit that by mentioning the "speculation," they were participating in "outing," the egregious activity whose name they'd coined six years earlier. Even though they most certainly were.

In truth, when it comes to public figures and the media, whether we use the term "outing" or not, the closet is beginning to collapse in on itself, no longer a safe refuge for the queer and famous. One reason is simply that gay and lesbian journalists themselves are out of the closet for the first time in significant numbers in newsrooms across the country. They often push editors to deal with the issue of outing with more depth and to grapple with the celebrity closet. Gay activists, too, whether radicals like those in Queer Nation in the early 1990s or the more mainstream types like the Gay and Lesbian Alliance Against Defamation, have had an impact on the media over the past six years, demanding a more complex treatment of issues like public figures' private sexuality. By using the Internet to get past the filters of the media, activists will also continue to get such information to the public without editors censoring them, as the DOMA outings demonstrated. And much of the media, afraid of being left in the dust, will increasingly feel compelled to pick up on this information.

In 1993, Tom Goldstein, dean of the Graduate School of Journalism at the University of California, Berkeley, called outing a "fleeting phenomenon." That was wishful thinking at best, and embarrassingly naïve coming from a journalism school honcho. For it's quite clear that as homosexuality becomes more accepted, outing becomes more acceptable. The two phenomena are inextricably linked. As pop stars and TV celebrities like Melissa Etheridge, Amanda Bearse, k.d. lang, Dan Butler, Elton John, RuPaul, and others continue to come out and not see their careers ruined (but in fact enhanced); as politicians (like three of the four openly gay members of the 104th Congress and dozens of state and local elected officials) announce their homosexuality and are reelected; and as average Americans keep coming out every day to their family, friends, and coworkers, the idea that revealing a person's homosexuality is a terrible action that automatically ruins his or her life begins to wear thin.

More to the point, as straight public figures, from Hollywood stars to Washington political candidates, continue to have their personal lives dissected, glamorized, and criticized, held up to the public without their consent, it's only a matter of time before the media are viewed as giving gay public figures "special treatment" by respecting their closets. If, after all, an unmarried heterosexual starlet must contend with media speculations and revelations about her undisclosed pregnancy, why must the media respect a comedian's wishes not to have her undisclosed lesbianism speculated about, particularly if it will no longer ruin her career? Some people might consider it a dubious honor to have the most intimate aspects of our lives put under a microscope in a media-obsessed culture. And in some ways they're right. But a community such as this one, whose greatest liability is invisibility, will always have a paradoxical relationship with the press. Like it or not, the increased acceptance of outing is a measure of our success.

Out, **December 1996**

HOMO FOR THE HOLIDAYS

WE'D LEFT NEW YORK far behind—twenty of us in a Winnebago, blazing down the roads of "Amish Country," in rural south-eastern Pennsylvania. The Amish, an orthodox religious sect who separated from the Mennonites in the late seventeenth century, live today not much differently than their ancestors: Men till the soil, women are shrouded from head to toe, and horse-and-buggy is their chosen means of transportation.

They lead a simple life. And we clearly do not: A glittering mob, many of us in sequined evening gowns and big hair in electric colors, we were—judging from the looks on the faces of many an Amish farmer—the queerest thing to barrel through Amish Country in a while.

But this was not my own version of *To Wong Foo*. This was my family.

We were going to a wedding. Uncle Tony was marrying a woman from a well-to-do, white Protestant family. The affair was to take place at her family's house in the woods, on the edge of Amish Country. And so, my Staten Island Italian family chartered a minibus, and took off for uncharted (to us, at least) territory.

In our family, weddings are usually glitzy evening events. There is of course the Catholic church service in the late afternoon, but the real celebration is a nighttime extravaganza in a crystal-chandeliered catering hall that goes at least until midnight. But an afternoon outdoor wedding? "It's ridiculous," Aunt Jeannie proclaimed as we pulled into a long driveway. "You only see this kind of thing on TV, on soap operas."

We arrived to find cocktails and light hors d'oeuvres, prompting Cousin Vito to comment under his breadth about the "cheap spread," and Aunt Rosie to exclaim more loudly, "Gee, I wish I woulda known—I woulda brought a lasagna!"

The service took place on a deck in the back of the house. On the left side sat the bride's family. They were mostly blond, dressed demurely: Men in khaki, beige, or light blue linen suits, women in white, pink or pale yellow day dresses. Our men, on the other hand, mostly wore dark pinstripe suits, and our women were in shining frocks of black, crimson, purple, and lime green. "They really dress terribly," my cousin Angela whispered to me as she checked out the bride's family. "No pizzazz."

A violinist played the Wedding March, as my uncle's wife-to-be was escorted down the aisle by her father. While the other side stood quietly admiring the bride, there was a scuffle on our side, as several people jockeyed for position, taking Polaroids. When the bride reached the place where the minister and the groom stood, there was a moment of silence. But that was soon pierced by a shriek from Grandma, who was sitting in back of me.

"Get outta here!" she howled, as all heads at the wedding turned around to look. She was waving her hands in front of her face. "There's a lot of bees around here," she said with a smile to the forty-odd faces staring at her. Indeed, for the remainder of the service, a bee colony hovered over my family's lacquered hair, and Grandma's would not be the last shriek to be heard.

Those are the moments when I truly love my family. They are the moments in which, no matter how alien from them I may have previously felt because of my homosexuality, our common background transcends any differences among us. Together, we flaunt our Staten Island-ness, and we revel in it. Rather than allowing ourselves to feel intimidated or inferior, we build our individual and collective self-esteem by focusing on the characteristics of our lives that we believe are not just equal to others but are actually better—more lively, more colorful, more liberated, whatever.

Ironically, it is also during those same moments that I sometimes become angry with my family for not completely getting my gayness. Why can't they see, I ask myself, that we gay people do exactly what they do in the face of people who might look down on us, loudly and proudly proclaiming who we are without shame? But homophobia is much more complicated than I'd ever imagined; just when I think my family—my parents in particular—have finally conquered their Italian Catholic demons, something tells me they've got a long way to go. This dilemma is heightened at various times, depending on what's going on in my life. And lately, it's been particularly acute, as I embark on bringing my new boyfriend home for the holidays.

As we all come to learn, coming out is not a one-day affair, it's a lifelong process. And many of us find that we as well as our families sometimes go back into the closet, in a manner of speaking, at different points in our lives. That's why, for me, going home for the holidays (or at any time), a quick but anxiety-ridden ferry ride from Manhattan to Staten Island, is a mixed bag, full of surprises. No matter how out I am publicly—and in my case that's pretty damn out—I never know if we're all going to be in the closet again when I get there, and if I have to once again bust my way out.

When my first book, *Queer in America,* was published in 1993, my parents were ecstatic. Two years earlier, they were still distraught that their son was queer, but like many parents whose emotions swing like a pendulum about a child's homosexuality, they were now "the most . . . supportive parents in America," as I wrote in the book's dedication. Upon my presenting it to them at a family function, they ran around the room showing the book to everyone; my mother even put a copy in the living-room window. Perhaps the national mood of the time had something to do with their enthusiasm: The president, not yet four months in office, was standing up for gay people (remember that?), and lesbians and gay men were the trend story of the minute, the news media momentarily going out of their way to put a positive spin on our lives.

But two years later, things had changed. And so, it seems, had my parents. When I went home last spring with my second book, *Outing Yourself,* my father's first question was, "Are you going to keep writing on this same topic?" What did he expect instead? That I would "go to Hollywood and write a screen-play" about "regular" people's lives. My mother said the book was "very nice," then went into her bedroom and stuck it in a drawer. I was ready to explode—not just about the book, but also about their lack of interest in other aspects of my life. Unlike with my three brothers, my parents rarely ask me about my friends, and never ask about boyfriends. For all practical purposes, my life as a gay man seems to be in the shadows.

If the irony of the situation was lost on them, it wasn't lost on me: I had just written a book telling other people how to come out, and my own parents and I were back in the closet.

I soul-searched and I came to realize that I was as responsible for this situation as they were. Unlike with their heterosexual kids, there are no rules around this for my parents to follow. No one has told them how much they're supposed to ask about a homosexual son's life, and I hadn't given them enough to go on.

My brother Frank, who, like my two other brothers, has been very accepting, offered succinct advice: "If you don't push 'em, they ain't gonna move."

He was right. My parents hadn't met—or heard much about—any of my friends since college, and in the last six years I hadn't had a boyfriend to speak of, let alone to introduce them to. Except perhaps for carefully selected highlights of my professional life, I'd not brought up even the most mundane personal matters for discussion. Even when I'd gone public in the media about a personal issue, my parents rarely mentioned seeing it, and I rarely referred to it. On the one or two occasions when I did bring it up, the discussion was short and tense.

Part of my motivation for withholding or not dwelling on information about my life, I realized, has been due to the internalized homophobia that I, like all gay people, battle every day. It's true that most adult children, straight or gay, are highly selective when it comes to sharing information about their lives with parents. But most heterosexuals do bring home the basics: who their friends are and what they're like, who they're seriously dating, living with, or marrying. On the other hand, many gay people often don't share facts surrounding these aspects of our lives because we're not sure how they'll fly—because deep down maybe we're just a little bit (or a lot) embarrassed (or even ashamed) about them. We become hell-bent on breaking stereotypes; that often means going out of our way to show our families that we (and the people in our lives) are the same as them, not different. And that's where it starts: We go about censoring our lives to the point where we construct another closet.

I had some work to do. I called up my parents and invited them over to my apartment—where I've lived for two years but which they've never seen even though they live thirty minutes away. Then, over dinner at a nearby restaurant, I said, "You know, you rarely ask me about my life, and I realize that's partially my fault, but I'd like you to ask. I want you to know that I've been involved with someone special for a while now. His name is David."

"Well, I don't ask you about your personal life," my mother responded, a bit annoyed.

"From now on you can, okay?" I said. "David is a great guy, by the way, and I'd like you to meet him sometime in the future."

"Sure—" my father said.

"In the future," my mother interrupted nervously.

Since then, I've brought David to meet my father and my brothers, at their restaurant on Wall Street. And on the telephone I've mentioned David again and again to my mother, who becomes quite uncomfortable but is getting the message that, come the holidays, she's going to meet my new beau. Meanwhile, David and I are heading to Buffalo for his sister's Italian wedding. His family, a Buffalo version of my Staten Island brood, has been at this for quite some time (I'm not the first boyfriend he will have brought home), and seem much more comfortable with the idea. That gives me hope and encouragement.

Once in a while, I ask myself why on earth I'm putting myself through all of this stress. After all, it would be a lot easier to just drop my family entirely. I suppose I could answer that question by saying that I think it's each of our duties to work with our families so that collectively we'll battle homophobia on a grand scale. But that would be a whitewash (as accurate as the statement may be). The truth is, just when I'm disgusted with my family and am ready to throw in the towel, I think back to events like Uncle Tony's wedding. And I come to the realization that they may not be everybody's people, but they're *my* people.

Out, **January 1996**

TRANSGENDER NATION

"LET ME GIVE YOU a couple of sound bites—*write this down*," Riki Anne Wilchins commands me. She's sitting on the floor of her studio apartment in a well-kept prewar building in New York's Greenwich Village. A log is burning in the fireplace, but it is Wilchins who is highly combustible tonight. She begins by listing some of the events that Transexual Menace (one S, she insists)—a loosely organized group she helped found that now has "16 or so" chapters around the country—has been involved with in the two years since its inception.

One could argue that Menace activists have become the cutting edge of queer activism amid the lull from ACT UP and Queer Nation in recent years. They took on the "womyn-born—womyn only" policy at the annual lesbian-dominated

Michigan Womyn's Music Festival, camping outside the main gate each night until organizers finally allowed male-to-female (MTF) transsexual women into the festival last August. They participated with other groups in National Gender Lobby Day in Washington last October, speaking about their issues to any member of Congress who would listen. They demonstrated in Falls City, Nebraska, in May 1995 on the opening day of the trial of the murderer of Brandon Teena, a Nebraska youth who'd been beaten, raped, and killed by teenage boys, and then they picketed the *Village Voice* when lesbian journalist Donna Minowitz's report of the trial referred to Teena as a "lesbian" who passed as a boy rather than calling Teena "transgendered." Halfway into our interview, in fact, Wilchins, only half-jokingly, threatens to picket *me* if she is not pleased with what I write.

She becomes angry at times, in a right-on sort of way. "I find it ironic that this entire fucking movement was launched by a bunch of gender queers sitting in a third-rate bar right down the street from us—a bunch of leather dykes, transsexuals, and Third World people," she says emphatically, referring to the 1969 riots at the Stonewall bar. "And now they are the first ones shown the door now that the revolution is bearing some fruit, told that they're not included in this bill or that bill."

The bill she's talking about is the Employment Non-Discrimination Act (ENDA), championed by the Washington, D.C.–based Human Rights Campaign, the largest national gay and lesbian political organization. Although 133 representatives and 30 senators have pledged their support—as has Bill Clinton—it will probably take years before ENDA even approaches passage. The bill would outlaw discrimination based on "sexual orientation" in most housing and employment. But for Wilchins and other transgender activists that is not enough.

They believe that ENDA must also specifically outlaw discrimination based on "gender expression." That, she says, would cover people who are "transsexuals, nellie queens, leather dykes, cross-dressers, drag kings and drag queens, and diesels." As an umbrella to cover all these (and still other) groups, Wilchins uses the term *transgendered,* although its meaning and acceptance are not yet uniform.

The question is, Aren't all those transgendered people—"nellie queens," for example—covered under the term *sexual orientation?* No, Wilchins says. People may be fired from their jobs and gay-bashed not because of actual information about their orientation, she points out, but simply because they appear too "effeminate" or "butch" for their gender. She dismisses the notion that such actions are the result of *perceived* sexual orientation, and therefore would be covered by ENDA—she wants explicit language to include the transgendered, not implied protection. For that reason, Transexual Menace went head-to-head with HRC over the bill, picketing black-tie fund-raising dinners around the country. "[HRC executive director] Elizabeth Birch said to me 'Why are you doing this to us?' " Wilchins recalls, "and I said, 'That is not the question. The question is why do we still have to?' "

As Wilchins explains her concept of transgendered politics, I become convinced that the problem is not simply a visceral "transphobia" on the part of lesbians and gay men who can pass as straight, as she implies over and over again (though the charge can certainly be leveled at some gay conservatives). Rather it seems to me that twenty-seven years after Stonewall, most lesbian and gay people simply don't challenge traditional thinking about gender and transsexuality, In particular, most of us have not been exposed to the ideas put forth by today's transgender activists. To most self-identified lesbian and gay people, for example, ENDA should logically cover people who identify as gay, lesbian, or bisexual—and anyone discriminated against because they're *perceived* to be gay, lesbian, or bisexual. If someone is trangendered (by Wilchins's definition) and identifies as gay, lesbian, or bisexual, then they're already covered. Protecting transgendered people who identify as heterosexual would be a separate bill, a separate fight. Simple as that. But many transgender activists don't see it all so black and white. And their provocative ideas could have broad implications for the entire lesbian and gay movement, challenging what it means to be "gay," "lesbian," or "bisexual," and indeed calling into question whether "sexual orientation" even exists in any essential way.

To those who accept the traditional bipolar definition of gender—that is, that people are either male or female and adhere to clearly defined categories of sexual orientation (heterosexual, gay and lesbian, or bisexual)—which is *most* people, it's unfathomable that someone doesn't have a particular sexual orientation. But it is precisely what some transgender activists now argue.

"Most of us assume that there *is* gender; that there are only two categories of gender, and that we are (have the identity of) one or the other," writes the transsexual performance artist Kate Bornstein in *Gender Outlaw: On Men, Women, and the Rest of Us.* "We have a lot invested in this belief—it's very difficult for us to imagine ourselves genderless." Like Wilchins, Bornstein was born biologically male and had surgery to construct female genitalia; also like Wilchins, after a long road and a lot of self-reflection, Bornstein now says that she is neither a man nor a woman, neither heterosexual nor a lesbian (though both have called themselves lesbian in the past).

Many transgender activists have found arguments to bolster their beliefs in the work of the French deconstructionist philosophers and of American academics like Judith Butler, author of *Gender Trouble* ("I'm a Butler clone" Wilchins proudly exclaims). Using such works, the activists argue that gender— that is, the attributes assigned to "male" and "female"—is a social construction, and that this binary thinking effectively operates to keep people rigidly in place. By forcing all people into roles they may not like, this neat categorization works to the detriment of women (and, ultimately, many men) as well as queers, in the broadest sense of the word. Because this bipolar thinking is so ingrained in society, transgender activists argue, when a person rejects the gender he or she has been assigned, the societal pressure to choose the other gender is immense. There is no allowing for anyone who doesn't identify as either male or female. In that way, many transsexuals, following pre-vailing medical beliefs, claim to be "a man trapped in a woman's body" or "a woman trapped in a man's body," and then seek surgery to create or remove breasts and construct genitalia of the opposite gender. But by living their lives as a member of the "opposite" gender, some transgender activists would argue they are simply going from one cage to another, keeping the gender order in place. It's those who straddle the fence—not choosing either gender and often, but not always, rejecting surgery—who are truly disrupting the status quo, challenging the gender order, and working towards dismantling it.

Not surprisingly, these new ideas have had the effect of an intellectual atom bomb on the transsexual community. Many MTF and female-to-male (FTM) transsexuals are angry that their identities are being challenged, having believed for their whole lives in the idea of two genders, and that they truly were born into the wrong one. "This is the big split," says transgender activist Jess Bell, referring to the two camps of thought. Bell describes herself as "a butch lesbian who passes a very good amount of the time as a boy" and runs a support and activist group for transgendered people in her hometown of Burlington, Vermont. "I see it as the great divide that's really separating our community. I wouldn't say that it's generational —I know a lot of older transsexuals who do embrace [the new] ideas, and younger people who don't."

Sarah Chandler, who lives in a small New Hampshire town and used to describe herself as an MTF transsexual, has incurred the wrath of many transsexuals recently for calling her surgery "mutilation." She has been on the Sally Jessy Raphaël show ten times and has just finished a book, *Transcending Illusions*. "My old media, before the surgery, was all about how much I wanted the surgery, and how it was going to change my life," she says. "But now, my new media is about transcending our bodies. I realize I shouldn't have had [the surgery] because it's not really perfected. I'm not a man or a woman. A lot of transsexuals say 'I'm a woman.' Well, you're not a woman. You're as close to being a woman that a man will ever get, but you're not a woman. Now I'm under attack; they're saying I'm setting the movement back. But I can't keep lying."

A self-described FTM transsexual who is working on a doctoral dissertation at Brandeis University on the formation of FTM identities, Henry S. Rubin takes great umbrage at the term *mutilation* and has attacked the new activists' ideas about gender. He writes in the feminist publication *Sojourner* that French deconstructionism is misinterpreted by most transgender activists. He compares the current influence of academia on the transsexual movement to that exerted on lesbian-feminism in the 1970s, "when middle-class, feminist theorizing changed the face of lesbianism" and offered "only one righteous path. . . . All of this is done in the name of politics and without regard for the lived experiences of transsexuals."

Perhaps he has a point. At New York's Hetrick-Martin Institute for Lesbian and Gay Youth, on grimy Astor Place in New York's East Village, far from any ivory towers, I meet nineteen-year-old Francis Cornejo, who is currently taking female hormones and lives in a group home for queer youth in Brooklyn. She tells me, "I have been a woman trapped in a man's body. Right now I consider myself a transgendered person. If I have surgery, I will be a transsexual. But I am a woman and have known I am a woman from when I was very young." No amount of academic gender theory, it appears, will shake her from that belief.

The compromise between these opposing views is perhaps found in Leslie Feinberg, lecturer, political activist, and author of *Stone Butch Blues* and the just-published *Transgender Warriors.* "I don't really hold a socially constructionist view that *every* bit of our gender is socially constructed or that there is a biological determinant, in that we're all coded with DNA," she says. "I think it may well be an interaction between the two. For example, if gender expression and gender as a whole is all socially taught, why are there so many of us who don't learn it?"

What Feinberg does agree on with Riki Anne Wilchins, Jess Bell, and Kate Bornstein, is that the rejection by many transgender activists of the bipolar gender system throws much of the larger lesbian and gay movement up in the air. For without gender there isn't sexual orientation, which is, after all, determined by what gender one is sexually attracted to. For that reason, and for the sake of political expediency and unity, Bornstein believes we should drop terms such as *lesbian, gay,* and *bisexual,* and all go forth under the transgendered banner. She argues, like Wilchins, that "gay men and lesbians are more consciously excluded" for their visible gender expression than for their sexual practices—which, she says, usually happen behind closed doors. (Of course, whether straight people are more offended by visible transgender expression or by the mere *idea* of homosexual sex is a debatable point. Gay men and lesbians are being kicked out of the military not necessarily because they appear too effeminate or too butch, but because they have admitted or been accused of having homosexual sex. An acknowledgment of gay sex, even if a person seems to fit into the gender order, is clearly just as threatening as someone obviously transgendered.)

"For lesbians and gays to include transgendered people or indeed be included by them," Bornstein writes, "it would require that gays and lesbians admit to what amounts to their own transgender status. It would require that they question their definition of their sexual identity, which is currently based solely on the gender of their desired partners."

Other transgender activists take a more moderate approach. "I think that saying gender is a construction that needs to be eliminated is very forward, but it's not the reality we're in now, so I understand why some people get upset," says Craig Hickman, a transgendered performance artist who lives in Boston. "We're not going to tear down the walls of gender overnight—and we may never do that. But in my mind, looking at things in this way is like looking at our lives, of understanding ourselves."

Perhaps HRC, for one, is beginning to understand. Although the group is not lobbying in favor of rewording ENDA in the aftermath of the protests and meetings, HRC has officially dropped opposition to having the bill amended to include protection based on "gender expression" (something that transgender activists have convinced Senator James M. Jeffords of Vermont to sponsor). HRC executive director Elizabeth Birch also proposed a meeting between transgender activists and the

NOW Legal Defense and Education Fund to discuss the inclusion of transgendered people in laws that protect people on the basis of gender. And while testifying before Congress for reauthorization of the Hate Crimes Statistics Act, Birch argued that transgendered individuals, previously not mentioned in the bill, should be added.

But does standing shoulder to shoulder regardless of differences in our sexual (and gender) expressions mean that gay groups must constantly refer to our community as the "gay-lesbian-bisexual-transgendered movement" or "g/l/b/t"? I have argued against that in the recent past (incurring the wrath of some) in part because it does precisely the opposite of what many transgender activists profess is their goal; It puts us into neat categories, forcing people to choose which rigid definition they belong to, and scares away those who might not feel that they fit so neatly into one category.

Riki Anne Wilchins acknowledges this problem, and notes that we'll have to keep adding terms to the list because we'll never cover everyone: What about the "intersexed," for example, those now known as hermaphrodites? Having a separate identity is often just as important to the transgendered as it is to anyone else. "I don't think we should scrap [the terminology] at all," says Jess Bell. "I want to see all the terms. I think besides it would make some people invisible." Or as Francis Cornejo, the transgendered youth at Hetrick-Martin, told me, "I think it's important to always include the transgendered and the bisexuals, too. It's true that we're all part of the same family—there's a gay tree, like there is a family tree—but like in a family, we always have to remember that people have different names, and we always have to remember to mention everyone in the family."

Out, June 1996

QUEER IN A MILLION

WATCHING TELEVISION NEWS COVERAGE of the Million Man March, the historic if controversial gathering of black men on the mall in Washington, D.C., last October, momentarily brought me back to the 1993 March on Washington for Gay Rights. Men and women of every age, class, and color, and from every region of the country, came together on that April weekend to express one thing: Gay pride—whatever way they defined it. And that was enough, if only for one day, to powerfully unite people. I shared a cab at one point with a sixty-five-year-old lesbian from Kentucky whom I'd never met before yet with whom I had an exhilarating if brief conversation. By the end of our ride we were hugging each other and exchanging numbers. We still talk on the phone now and then, and inevitiably our chats brings us back to that empowering weekend.

A few weeks before that march, I'd had a conversation with a black lesbian acquantaince who pointed out her dilemma with gay-pride events such as the March on Washington. "A lot of my African-American friends have decided not to go to the march," she had told me. "They see it as a 'white gay' event, like most of the high-profile events in the gay community, which are organized for the most part by white, middle-class people for the sake of white, middle-class America." And yet, though she agreed with her friends' sentiments, she felt obliged—for the sake of black gay pride—to go to the march. "My feeling is that by staying home you only make things worse," she said. "By not going you only further the invisibility of African-American gays and lesbians—both in the white gay community and the straight world."

White gays and lesbians are rarely faced with such complex quandaries, pitting their sexual orientation against their race. For black gay men and lesbians, it's par for the course. Clearly, the Million Man March presented many black gay men and lesbians with a few basic dilemmas: Should they stay away in protest of the march's exclusion of black women, as well as the hate speech about gays, Jews, and others that has been spewed consistently by Nation of Islam leader Louis Farrakhan, who'd called the march over a year ago and remained one its most visible organizers? Or should they attend, both to show their solidarity with the plight of black men and to let it be known that black manhood doesn't only mean the heterosexual variety? In the end, some black gay men seized the day for themselves. And, for them, the march became an exercise in both gay visibility and black pride.

"I was told, 'You care more about black issues than gay

issues,' " says Gregory Adams, a black gay man, of the reaction from two white friends who approached him at a Dupont Circle gay bar a few hours after he had attended the Million Man March. "They assumed I was defending Farrakhan. They said, 'If he can convert you, then I'm worried about how much power he'll gain.' Those kinds of sentiments ran throughout the bar that night. These white men felt it appropriate to tell me which black leaders to support or not support, and then to challenge my allegiance to the gay community."

Like many black men, straight or gay, at the march, Adams says that his attendance was far from a show of support for Louis Farrakhan. At first, he hadn't planned on going because of the controversial leader's presence, but changed his mind as the event drew closer and as the march seemed to take on a greater significance than the man who called it. "I think [black gay men] belong right next to our straight brothers," he says, articulating one of the reasons he changed his mind. "We experience the same racism. I'm a black gay man who still can't get a cab in D.C."

There was no question that black gay men would be present at the march in droves. Depending on whose figures you used—both to calculate the exact number of men who would attend, as well as to figure out the percentage of the black male population that might be gay—you might have predicted that anywhere from 10,000 to 100,000 gay men would show up. But as in every other racial and ethic community, most would be invisible. As usual, it would take activists to provide a proud, openly gay contingent, distinguishable from their straight brothers.

Much of the black gay and lesbian activist community was, however, divided on whether or not to attend. "I understood the reasons for the importance of the march," says Donald Suggs, former media director of the Gay and Lesbian Alliance Against Defamation. "There are so many negative images—from O.J. to Michael Jackson—of black men in the media, and we needed to redefine the images, to show images that are more reflective of who we are. But any definition of me as an African-American man has to include black women. And I think it's really important for us as black gay men to define ourselves and not to accept any definition put out there, nor to assume we're included when we're not explicitly mentioned." Suggs followed the appeals of black feminists, women like sixties revolutionary Angela Davis, who had come out against the march.

But others decided the march presented an opportunity that was too great to pass up. "I realized the *absence* of gay activists was not going to make a dent in the numbers of people supporting the march, and that the *presence* of gay activists could make a difference in the way it affected the marchers," says Keith O. Boykin, executive director of the National Black Lesbian and Gay Leadership Forum (NBLGLF). With several other activists, Boykin spent the weeks leading up to the march negotiating with march organizers about getting an openly gay speaker as well as a person with AIDS on the platform. But a firm answer from march organizers didn't come until the very last minute, when no such speakers materialized. "I think that they were really thinking about it, and also trying to stall us," says Phil Wilson, founder of NBLGLF and currently executive director of AIDS Project Los Angeles. "They just didn't know what to do. There were definitely people who who were supportive, but there were also people who were uncomfortable and opposed to the idea."

The activists weren't about to let the absence of an openly gay speaker put a damper on their presence; perhaps it emboldened them, making it even more essential that they be visible. On the night before the march, several of them stayed up all night, preparing for the media and booking themselves and others on television morning-chat shows. "We went to Kinko's [copy center] and made fifty press kits, and we didn't get back to Keith Boykin's house until about 3:30 A.M., when we started putting the kits together and making phone calls," says Maurice Franklin, an entertainment management consultant from New York.

The group, which didn't have any official name (NBLGLF voted not to endorse the march, but to encourage members to go on their own), kicked off their morning with a rally on a street corner several blocks from the mall at which 150 gay men, and a few lesbians, attended. Their guerrilla media blitz had paid off: As the black lesbian poet Sabrina Sojourner and other speakers addressed the crowd, dozens of reporters and photographers surrounded them. Soon after the rally, the group began marching down Pennsylvania Avenue toward the mall, many wearing T-shirts identifying them as gay or holding signs proclaiming it loudly and clearly. They didn't know what to expect, and indeed some thought it might not be safe for a bunch of gay men to be crashing what some straight men might see as their own party.

"Many of us had talked about getting beat down walking onto the mall," recalls Maurice Franklin. "I was prepared for whatever happened. If I had to fight I would fight. But that didn't happen." Instead of homophobia, Franklin says, the group was almost universally met with what some said can only be described as expressions of warmth and brotherhood. "We first started chanting 'Black! black! gay! gay!' " he remembers. "Then we started doing 'Gay men of African descent!' and we were jumping up and down and hollering. People were honking their horns, and cheering, and saying 'Represent!' People were taking pictures, and some of them would put their fists up in support.

And when we got to the mall it was just overwhelming. I'm not trying to dismiss the issue of homophobia in our community, because clearly it exists. But on that day, on that mall, I felt like I knew what it was like to be in the Promised Land. I felt safe, as if I was in a perfect world for one day."

"People moved aside—it was like Moses parting the Red Sea," says Russell Thornhill, who came from Los Angeles, where he is director of training for a Mexican restaurant chain. "We proudly walked down the center of the mall. Some people gestured the power sign, putting their fists in the air. You heard men screaming and yelling with excitement and enthusiasm."

Several of the black gay men who marched openly that day say they felt as if they had put a dent in people's beliefs, and perhaps helped them see and accept gay men for who they are. "During the course of the day, all the barriers, different religious backgrounds, different beliefs, all faded away," recalls Gregory Adams. "There were men who came over and showed solidarity with us by putting their hands on our clenched fists."

And some believe they reached out to those throngs of gay men who were at the march but who had not yet taken those first steps out of the closet. "I think part of what we did helped give other men a good feeling because they saw men who were proud of who they are, and that does affect them because they then feel good about themselves," says Thornhill. "People have to walk their own journey, and if we can stand up and help the 100,000 who might have been present to see us and to say to themselves, 'Well, I'm okay,' then we did our job."

Out, **February 1996**

THE SECRET HISTORY OF MORMONS

THOUGH IMMACULATE AND WHITE, Temple Square—spiritual center of the Mormon Church in the heart of downtown Salt Lake City—has a dark feel to it. Despite the bright and friendly smiles from welcoming churchwomen, and the whimsical, spired temple itself, looking like something from Disney's Magic Kingdom, the unyielding uniformity of the place is a tip-off that the Church of Jesus Christ of Latter-day Saints (LDS) doesn't tolerate in the slightest those of us who tread on life's sexual outskirts. There is a rich history to this animosity— a history that paradoxically begins with the Mormon Church's onetime support for same-sex affection.

D. Michael Quinn, a historian who was excommunicated in

1992 for his writings on women and the Mormon priesthood, has written a controversial new book recounting that history, *Same-Sex Dynamics Among Nineteenth-Century Americans: A Mormon Example* (University of Illinois Press). Quinn relates how in 1959, in the wake of the extreme homophobia of the McCarthy era, elders of the church gathered to discuss what they termed "the growing problem in our society of homosexuality." Shortly after that meeting, the Mormon-founded Brigham Young University in nearby Provo began a program of aversion therapy to "cure" male homosexuals. Suspected queers referred to the program were put in a dark room and shown erotic photos of both men and women and encouraged to masturbate while viewing the images of women. If they got an erection at the sight of the male erotica, however, they were jolted for eight long seconds with a 1,600-volt charge via electrodes connected to their arms.

Don Harryman attended BYU in the early 1970s and went through the aversion-therapy program. "The way the Mormons viewed it, [homosexuality] was practically worse than being a murderer, and it was spoken about often," he tells me. "I was desperate to change my sexuality." A school psychologist promised that aversion therapy would do the trick. "They have an instrument that you put on [your penis] that measures an erection. The shock would come to your arm randomly, [and it was] very painful." At first, the therapy seemed to work. "I hadn't ever had any sex [with a man] to begin with," Harryman recalls, "and I just got used to not thinking about it." But the "cure" didn't last long, Harryman notes: "Six months later, a new roommate moved in and I fell in love and was sexual with him within twenty-four hours. It was like the lights going on and me saying, 'Wow, that was all a sham!' "

While BYU abandoned electroshock treatments for

homosexuals long ago, Harryman—who now lives in Hawaii, where he is involved in the Hawaii Equal Rights Marriage Project—claims that some church leaders as recently as two years ago were quietly referring people to outside doctors who perform electroshock therapy. And the Mormon Church today promotes counseling and group therapy aimed at "curing" Mormon men and women who have same-sex desires. "The church turned my life upside down," says an ex-Mormon lesbian who lives in Ogden, Utah, and who left the church two years ago. "I spent years in counseling with church-approved therapists who had me believing that the gay lifestyle was immoral, that being a lesbian was terrible, and that I could really cure myself."

It wasn't always this way. According to historian Quinn's illuminating new book, same-sex love and intimacy, expressed in a variety of nonerotic ways, was common among the Mormons and throughout America in the nineteenth century. Sexual relations between people of the same gender were also common and, while technically "sinful," seemed to be understood as a fact of life—heterosexual adultery was of graver concern. Some prominent Mormon men and women even lived much of their lives involved in romantic and even sexual relationships with people of the same sex, Quinn contends. First of all, he stresses, the terms "homosexual," "gay," "lesbian," and "bisexual" did not exist when the church was founded. There was the notion of same-sex erotic behavior, Quinn notes, but there did not exist a classification of people considered same-sex oriented. (Quinn himself eschews such labels. "I was married and have four children, and so I feel I'm part of a complicated interaction," he tells me. "I don't define myself as 'bisexual' because I don't have an equal attraction to both genders. I am overwhelmingly attracted to men.")

A Yale graduate and a former professor of history and

director of the graduate program at BYU (he resigned in 1988), Quinn argues that same-sex intimacy was accepted and even encouraged by many nineteenth-century American social groups, including leading Mormons. Church founder Joseph Smith in 1842 went against traditional biblical teaching by preaching that God destroyed Sodom for "rejecting the prophets," rather than for sexually inappropriate behavior (although Smith's interpetation was later replaced with a more antihomosexual one). Smith, a polygamist, once wrote that male friends "should lie down on the same bed at night locked in each other's embrace talking of their love," something he himself did. At about the same time, in 1839, a twenty-seven-year-old Mormon, Elizabeth Haven, wrote to her Mormon second cousin Elizabeth Bullard, "If I could sleep with you tonight, [I] think we should not be very sleepy . . . at least I could converse all night and have nothing but a comma between sentences, now and then." Indeed, women who were companions did sleep with each other often, as did men.

Such same-sex relations were for the most part nonerotic, Quinn argues, but acceptance of this intimacy may have made life easier for those who engaged discreetly in same-sex sexual activity. In perhaps the most controversial account in his book, Quinn reveals that Evan Stephens, director of the Mormon Tabernacle Choir from 1890 through 1916 and a lifelong bachelor, spent much of his life with a series of male companions, relationships lasting a few months to several years. His "boy chums," as he called them, were choir members, mostly in their teens, and all went on to marry women.

Stephens's appreciation for the male form was no secret: He wrote in an LDS publication of "the picturesque manliness" of the choir's uniform, of "those coatless and [suspenderless] costumes worn by the men. What freedom and grace they gave, what full manly outlines to the body and chest, what a form to admire they gave to the creature Man." Indeed, Stephens regularly expressed his love for his various male companions in LDS publications. It raised no eyebrows. In 1916, at age sixty-two, Stephens gave up his twenty-six-year career to move to New York to be with an eighteen-year-old described by another "boy chum" as a "blond Viking who captured the eye of everyone as a superb specimen of manhood." From what he termed "Gay New York" (the word gay had by then been adopted by New York homosexuals), Stephens wrote letters back to Utah about wandering through Central Park looking for "some sort of companionship."

Stephens was one of several prominent early Mormons who Quinn believes was probably (although not definitely) sexually active with members of his own gender. Other Mormons of the time, though not as prominent, were more definitively homosexual. In a chapter titled "The Earliest Community Study of Lesbians and Gay Men," Quinn recounts the work of Mildred Berryman, a lesbian who studied and interviewed gay men and women in Salt Lake City in the early 1900s. Her landmark study showed that even in the heartland and the West, homosexuals were then finding each other and establishing communities, their affectional preferences sometimes known and tolerated by heterosexual friends and family. Even the law was more lenient to those who engaged in sex with those of their own gender. Utah did not even have laws outlawing sodomy until the United States government imposed them on the region, Quinn writes, and once the laws were established, nineteenth-century Mormon leaders and judges "were more tolerant of homoerotic behavior than they were of every other nonmarital sexual activity," which was punished more harshly.

It's ironic, to say the least, that a church that began with its founder promoting the idea of men sleeping together would, 150 years later, be promoting electroshock therapy to "cure" people who expressed a desire for same-sex intimacy. By 1976, Mormon Apostle Boyd K. Packer was holding up as a role model a young male missionary who had gay-bashed a fellow male missionary who had supposedly made a sexual advance. "Somebody had to do it," Packer said.

As I reported in this column in March, the economically powerful and politically influential Mormon Church is today a driving force in the campaign to push back gay rights in America. Utah, where more than 90 percent of the state legislators are Mormon, was the first state to explicitly outlaw same-sex marriage, and, as Elise Harris reported in these pages in June ("Shotgun Wedding"), the Mormon Church may also be backing efforts to stop same-sex marriage from becoming legal in Hawaii. But Quinn's work is more than just an account of the evolution of homophobia in Mormon society: It suggests that much of the homophobia in America may be of relatively recent origin, and it counters religious conservatives' contention that same-sex intimacy has always been unacceptable in Western faith. "I think that the findings of the book provide a way of seeing that an inflexible point of view about sexuality really doesn't relate to American culture as a culture," Quinn says. "These battle lines simply didn't exist 100 years ago. America as a culture was in the past more able to accept a certain kind of intimacy on same-sex issues than America is today."

Out, **September 1996**

LEAVE MY KID ALONE!

"Usually, when people harass me, I just give them an equal amount of harassment back," openly gay sixteen-year-old William Wagner, a student at Fayetteville High School in Fayetteville, Arkansas, tells me. When people have called him a *faggot*, for example, he has ridiculed them for their lack of imagination. "I say to them, 'Try *fairy* or *queer*, something with more spice,'" he explains. "'Don't you have any creativity?' I ask them. 'Why don't you use a thesaurus?' I make a carnival of their taunts. I undermine their taunts. If people are going to be that way to me, I'm going to take them down also." So when Brad Hufford, a school bully, charged up to William in the cafeteria last year when they were both attending Woodland Junior High, calling him a *faggot* and raising his fists, William employed his usual strategy, making a fool out of the guy. "I put my leg up and he racked himself, rammed his balls into my foot, and he pretty much lost most of his wind and fell to the floor. And ever since then he was intent on getting me." Last December, several youths, one of them allegedly Brad Hufford, finally did get William. He was on his way to the Hog Wash Laundry with some friends when a blue pickup truck pulled up and some boys got out and jumped him. They beat him up savagely a few blocks from Fayetteville High while yelling antigay slurs. William suffered a broken nose, bruised kidney, bruising on his back and other parts of his body, and scrapes and cuts on his knees.

Local law enforcement and newspapers took the beating seriously: Brad and another youth identifed by William were arrested as adults and charged with suspicion of second-degree battery. In one of the few times that many people in northwest Arkansas can ever remember, the local paper used the word "homophobia."

William had been out to his parents since he was fourteen, but he'd refrained for the most part from telling his mother about ongoing abuse in junior high because, he says, "I didn't want to worry her." But Carolyn Wagner often saw the bruises on her son's body, and friends of William's told her what was going on, prompting her to ask William about it and then complain to the school's principal.

"My husband and I were told many times—by the principal, by the vice principal, by the counselors—that if William would just ignore the harassment, that it would go away," she says. "They saw William as the problem. One time I was told by the vice principal that William had made his choice. Over a two-year period, I can't count how many times I'd spoken to Evelyn Marbury [the principal]."

On one occasion, Carolyn Wagner was summoned to the school after William walked off campus in the middle of a school day. "He got so upset," she recalls, explaining the circumstances. "On the bus returning from a field trip that day, a group of kids put signs on the windows saying 'Help us! Willie's raping us!' William's dog had just been killed, run over by a car, and the boys taunted him on the bus by saying he killed the dog by performing sexual acts on it."

She takes a breath and continues. "I was the angriest at this particular incident because William was punished for walking off campus. The principal said there was no excuse for my son walking off campus. His punishment was that he had to go to school on a Saturday for half a day. And I was told that it was none of my business whether or not the other children received any consequences because of the harassment."

Since the beating in December, however, officials at Fayetteville High School, where both William Wagner and Brad Hufford now attend school, have been more responsive than those at Woodland Junior High. Carolyn Wagner says that the vice principal became genuinely alarmed after she spoke to him; he addressed all of the teachers in front of her, letting it be known that antigay harassment was not to be tolerated. Now that she has the ears of school officials, Carolyn Wagner is pushing for a school policy against sexual harassment based on sexual orientation. "I'm also trying to get them to implement a curriculum of tolerance that must address all diversities," she says, "not just sexual orientation, but race, gender, handicap, socioeconomic status, et cetera, and to address bullying when it is present."

Many Fayetteville students, too, seem more receptive, perhaps seeing how the media, the police, and, most important, school administrators responded. "I've all of a sudden become kind of like a local martyr," William says, slightly weary of all the attention. "I'm kind of over it now. The paper randomly went picking out people who said they knew me, and I didn't even know these people and they were saying, 'Oh, he's a cool guy—a bit flamboyant, but he was a good friend of mine.' And it's like, I'm not really all that flamboyant. I mean, I'm a flashy dresser and all, but I've only done drag in school, like, twice."

For many of us long out of high school, William Wagner's story simultaneously resonates with us and seems utterly foreign. We know all too well the experience of being taunted and beaten up in school, and when we hear about a kid being called a faggot or a dyke by other kids, haunting memories surface. And yet, the idea of being out of the closet in school with the support of our parents—in the middle of Arkansas, no less—seems unthinkable to us. And for the majority of gay and lesbian teens in America today, isolated and closeted, being out of the closet is still unthinkable. But for a great many others, the world is changing rapidly. They're at the cutting edge of the gay-rights movement—and, most remarkably, their parents are right behind them.

We still have a long way to go, of course, but advances in addressing the problems of gay and lesbian youth in the past decade have been astonishing. In cities like New York, where the Hetrick-Martin Institute for Lesbian and Gay Youth provides gay kids a safe and comfortable alternative—the city-funded Harvey Milk High School—those advances began in the 1980s. But now support systems for gay and lesbian teens are developing beyond the major cities and within the countless public and private school systems where straight and gay students attend school together. The Gay, Lesbian, and Straight Teachers Network (GLSTN), for example—a group of students and teachers fighting homophobia—was founded in 1990 and now has over sixty chapters in places like Kalamazoo, Michigan, and Anchorage, Alaska. Even now, GLSTN (pronounced "glisten") is gearing up for its first national conference in Salt Lake City, March 21 to 23—three days of organizing workshops for gay and straight students, teachers, parents, and activists from around the country. In-school activism has clearly joined our biggest causes. The hitch is, when it comes to gay youth, the people most directly affected—the students—need adult allies to accomplish their goals. Unlike, say, those working to ban antigay discrimination in the workplace or to legalize same-sex marriage, the adult gay men and lesbians working within a group like GLSTN are fighting not for their own rights, but for the rights of the next generation and, by extension, for future of the entire gay-rights movement. With no direct payback for adults, such work takes, as GLTSN executive director Kevin Jennings puts it, a certain amount of "altruism."

Of course, there are adults who are directly affected by the harm done to gay and lesbian youth in homophobic schools; besides the teachers and administrators, Parents, Families and Friends of Lesbians and Gays, well-known as PFLAG, is a national group made up mostly of straight people, and it's the organization that many young gay people turn to first for help and advice. Founded in 1981, PFLAG now has a whopping 425 chapters throughout the United States, and in recent years it has aggressively transcended the stereotypical image of moms and dads meeting in coffee klatches to offer gentle comfort for each other and for their children. It was PFLAG, for example, that directly took on the Christian Coalition last year when it created public-service TV ads linking Pat Robertson's nasty, homophobic rantings to the gay-bashing of our youth on the streets. Robertson's lawyers coerced stations into suppressing the ads, but the resulting publicity reached a national audience. Mom and Dad have taken the battle for their kids to the next level.

"I think most people turn to PFLAG as a support group," says Leslie Zucker, a PFLAG mom who lives in Springfield, New Jersey. "The emotional piece is the big piece of what PFLAG does and what brings people in. But I think a lot of people stay on and become active in the political arena." And there are, of course, parents who are themselves gay and lesbian, whether they've got kids from a straight marriage or have conceived or adopted children as openly gay adults. The children of the first wave of the so-called "lesbian baby boom" have been in elementary school for a few years now. Fearful of their children experiencing harassment because of their parents' sexual orientation, gay and lesbian parents are often actively involved in school issues, especially fighting antigay harassment. Soon after William Wagner's case became public, for example, a lesbian mother went to the papers to discuss how her heterosexual daughter was also being harassed at Fayetteville High School because of her mother's sexual orientation.

And where are straight parents in Middle America finding the strength to back up their kids against often daunting opposition? Perhaps the explosion of gay images and issues in the media throughout the country in recent years has helped to jump-start this parents' crusade to help their queer kids—kids who seem irrepressible about their sexual orientation. "There are now enough positive images of lesbians and gay men [in the media], and it's now become a question of integrity," says David Buckel, a staff attorney at Lambda Legal Defense and Education Fund in New York. Buckel represented Jamie Nabozny, the young man who sued his Ashland, Wisconsin, school district in federal court for failing to protect him, despite his and his parents' pleas, against repeated antigay violence and harassment. In a highly publicized out-of-court settlement, the school district agreed to pay Nabozny $900,000 in damages. "Jamie simply refused to deny he was gay," Buckel says. Along with Kelli Petersen, whose Gay-Straight Alliance prompted the antigay Utah legislators to ban all high-school clubs, Nabozny has become an example for millions of gay and lesbian teens that they can and should be out of the closet.

"I have friends who are trying [the closeted] tactic, and that may be right for them, but it's not for me," William Wagner says, expressing an increasingly familiar sentiment. "I am who I am, and lying about it is not going to get me jack shit. If I stay in the closet, well, that is such a dysfunctional state."

Fortunately for William, his parents are among an increasing number of heterosexual moms and dads who are accepting the simple fact that their children are gay or lesbian. While it's true that there are still far too many parents who reject their queer kids and, in the worst-case scenario, throw them out of their homes—according to one study, a chilling 26 percent of gay teens are forced out by their families—others are going to bat for lesbian and gay kids, confronting the homophobia in America's schools. The parents of today's average sixteen-year-old are between thirty-five and forty-five years of age, baby boomers who came of age during and after the post-Stonewall gay-rights movement. Many have known openly gay men and lesbians for a long time, and though it's a shock to find out their own kid is gay, it's not entirely alien to them.

"He told us when he was fourteen, and it hit like a ton of bricks," Carolyn Wagner says. "His dad and I are Catholic, but we had not bought the package of bologna by some of the organized religions. We had founded a camp for children with AIDS and cancer. So we met a lot of gay people through that work. And I met gay people through my job—I was a registered nurse. We had cookouts, and a gay couple would come over the house and they would hug and I didn't think anything of it. . . . It's different when it's your own child, however. But we got past the initial shock, and then we couldn't read up on it enough."

Together, William and his parents attempted to figure out how he could best deal with his homosexuality at school. "His father and I said, 'Be careful. There are people in this world who do not understand and who will hurt and kill people who are different just because they're different,' " she explains. "But he would not listen. His feeling was that it wasn't anything to be ashamed of. He felt he should not be any more careful or fearful than his sister was when she noticed boys. He at first agreed with his dad and me that he would not just go into a classroom and just say, 'Hey, I'm gay.' But when he was confronted with it, he didn't deny it, and when the word got around, he became a target. And that's when I became a reluctant activist."

Forty-one-year-old Bob Nabozny, Jamie's dad, is a carpenter who grew up in Ashland, Wisconsin, where Jamie's family still lives, a town with a population of 8,000. But even there, he says, "I've known a few gay people in town all my life. But I thought it was all show, a way for them to get attention. They were out, mostly older men. One passed away from AIDS here about five years ago. He was a bartender here in town, and he didn't hold anything back. I didn't have a problem with him. But this was my kid. It was really hard. My first thought was, 'God, it can't be my kid.' That went on for quite a while, probably about a year or so. After Jamie . . . started bringing his [gay and lesbian] friends up and I listened to their life stories, I realized, 'My God, this is real stuff.' And I realized, 'Wow, I've got to accept this or else I'm going to lose my son.' "

Jamie's mother, Carol Nabozny, has a brother who is gay. "That helped," she says. "I think I was one of the first ones [my brother] told. I was shocked at first. That was about seventeen years ago. He was somewhere in his mid-twenties. He had married twice and had a child by his second wife. But it didn't work. He decided to tell his family he was gay and live openly."

Bob and Carol Nabozny went through a situation similar to that of the Wagners, knowing their son was gay but not at first aware of the brual harassment he was suffering—he'd once been beaten in a school bathroom and urinated on while on the floor—the kind of harassment that led Jamie to attempt suicide several times. After they learned of the abuse, they went to school administrators to demand that action be taken to protect their son; like the Wagners, they were met with little sympathy and no real action.

Jamie's parents eventually helped their son launch his historic lawsuit, founded a PFLAG chapter in Ashland, and marched in the Gay Pride parade in Minneapolis. Like Jamie himself, a leader in the burgeoning gay-youth movement, the Naboznys, the Wagners, and many more, perhaps, represent the next wave of the gay-rights movement, when moms and pops and even grandmas and grandpas in great numbers head into the streets—and down to the local school-board meetings and the principal's office—to fight for their kids. In that way, their actions are not much different from the parents who eventually took to the streets during the antiwar movement, standing up for their sons who were in Vietnam or fighting the draft, helping to turn our staid images of moms and dads into one of united families fighting for justice. As Carolyn Wagner put it, they're "reluctant activists."

"I don't know if I'd call myself an activist yet," Carol Nabozny says modestly. "I'd like to do more, but I have a problem speaking in front of crowds. Jamie's going to be getting a Lambda Liberty Award in New York in May, and he wants me to go and say a few words. I will try. This will be the first time I've actually been there when he's accepted an award. He's come a long way. And so have we."

Out, **March 1997**

COMING HOME TO THE SOUTH

"I'VE LIVED IN NEW YORK City and Tampa, Florida, and I've traveled quite a bit," says Damien Hardin, who now lives in Nashville, her hometown, where she is a carpenter and bounty hunter. "But Tennessee is my home. This is the most peaceful, calm, serene place you can possibly be. You can get up and see the grass and the country, and enjoy a change of seasons. The crime is not as high as most places—and the places where I've been, whoa, there's crime!"

A handsome African-American ex-Marine in her thirties with a gorgeous set of muscles—the lesbian comic Mimi Gonzalez, from the stage at Nashville Pride this year, called Hardin "the dyke Tom of Finland"—Hardin is also often called upon to work security for visitors to Nashville. That's how we met: She acted as my bodyguard on my book-tour stop there. Needless to say, I felt safe. Sometimes, however, her clients aren't so gay-friendly.

"I've sometimes had to protect people I don't like—senators and other people like that—but it's part of the job," she says. "If they have had a problem with my being a lesbian, I have told them, 'Look, you have a choice. Do you want to live or die? Because my sexual preference doesn't make any difference in how I'm going to do my job.' "

But is Nashville a comfortable place to be openly gay? "Any place is a good place to be gay—if you live your life truthfully," Hardin replies. "It's difficult as hell here, yes. This is the Bible belt. You can't go more than thirty feet without hitting a church. But we're all trying to get to God in our own way, so that does not bother me. As time has gone by, yes, it has gotten more accepting. There used to be harder times, when you watched everything you said just to keep your job. Each year, I've watched Nashville Pride grow. And the younger folks— you see them coming out, and they've got more going on than we've ever had."

A lot of gay men and lesbians who grew up in the South have left their hometowns over the years, often for big cities in the Northeast and the West, or to Atlanta, the South's own growing metropolis. It's not always to escape homophobia: Some people crave that fast-paced urban life. But for a lot of gay people who grew up there, like Damien Hardin, the South is their true home, the place they come back to—or never leave at all.

"I never really found it to be more homophobic," says Kevin Snow, a thirty-eight-year-old activist and stand-up comic, talking about his home, Birmingham, Alabama. Snow bristles at big-city gay and lesbian activists and journalists who look upon gay people in the South with a sense of pity and sorrow, as if they were somehow deluding themselves. He points out that the vast majority of states—thirty-nine, in fact, including such supposedly tolerant places like New York and California—do not have antidiscrimination laws protecting gay men and lesbians. Yes, he notes, there are still sodomy statutes on the books in many Southern states that activists must work diligently to overturn. And yes, there are homophobic religious leaders, antigay media bias, and ugly gay-bashings. But, Snow says firmly, he's seen the same or worse in all the various cities around the country he lived in during the twenty years before he returned to Birmingham, in 1995. "I found more homophobia expressed in Kansas City and Los Angeles," he comments with a chuckle. "Nobody would be homophobic toward me here—I'm related to all of the rednecks!"

In a way, Alabama's reputation for intolerance has long made it a magnet for civil-rights activism. It was in Birmingham thirty-four years ago that four young black girls were killed in a racist church bombing, and it was from Selma to Montgomery that Martin Luther King, Jr. led the historic Freedom March in 1964. This year, in a throwback to the city's reactionary past, a Birmingham television station earned the dubious distinction of being the only ABC affiliate to ban the *Ellen* coming-out episode, garnering a lot of negative publicity for the city and the South in general. But Snow feels the resulting media hype overshadowed a growing sense of inclusiveness among a lot of people in Alabama.

"The South certainly has a reputation for racism and homophobia," he says. "But we have a lot of progressive people here as well, and I really do love it here in Birmingham, which I think is very accepting. I find the reaction very funny that I get from activists around the country who are coming to visit. I've had people ask me, before they come, if they're going to be shot. When they get here, they're quite surprised."

Snow makes a good point: What we don't often hear about in places like Alabama are the less hyperbolic changes of attitude, which occur beneath the media's radar. Elliot Jones, a Birmingham AIDS activist, proudly tells how his family has learned to deal with his homosexuality and his having AIDS. "My father used to be the press secretary to George Wallace," he says, referring to the conservative Alabama governor who carried much of the South when he ran as an ultraconservative third-party presidential candidate in 1968. "And now [my dad]'s an AIDS activist in Huntsville."

Those are the stories that inspire Kevin Snow. A bright man with a big smile and a hearty laugh, Snow's positive attitude turns any adversity to his advantage. In February, for example, he helped arrange that *Ellen*'s coming-out show be received by satellite for viewing at the famous downtown theater where Nat King Cole was once denied permission to perform. The screening drew more than 2,500 people, a record gathering for any gay and lesbian event in Alabama, and it galvanized the community: Many people came out of the closet that night, Snow says, willing to be interviewed on television for the first time. The *Ellen* showing garnered Birmingham's gay community local and national attention, the kind that can lead to long-lasting visibility.

"We've gotten tons and tons of media coverage," he says, as we stand in stately and pristine Rushton Park, the sight of this year's Birmingham Pride celebration. "And the media people struck up friendships with us. They've never covered us for Gay Pride before. But here they are this year, interviewing everybody."

Pride in Birmingham is indeed what the first Gay Prides in

New York and San Francisco must have been like almost thirty years ago: a few hundred people marching through neighborhood streets, receiving jeers as well as distant smiles and waves. There's a sense of protest as well as celebration, a feeling that you're confronting onlookers' homophobia as well as offering some support to closeted people peering out of their windows. "It's the usual thing," Snow says, explaining the huge number of gay people still reluctant to participate. "People afraid of their families seeing them. Most gay people won't even go to bars around here, let alone come to Pride."

The paradox of increased acceptance and visibility while the vast majority of the gay community remains at least somewhat closeted exists in most of the South, Damien Hardin says. "This area is East Nashville, but we call it Gay Highland Heights," she says laughing, referring to Nashville's largely straight upscale neighborhood. Not quite Highland Heights' mansions, East Nashville's houses are nevertheless well-kept, colorful, and, well, queer, with touches of lavender paint and rainbow flags. "It's neat here because we've taken an old district and upgraded it by taking it back to the old traditional," Hardin says. But many gay people live elsewhere, and differently. "Then there's what we call Gay Redneck," says Hardin, "and that part of town, well, they're all closeted. You got these gay people who are the most prejudiced, true mountain-country people. I'm like, How in the hell can you be gay and be prejudiced? They go through the whole charade of acting like they're straight. Everything a redneck would do, they do it too. When it's time to party, they leave that world for a while and then go out to the gay bars. But they never, ever come to the meetings or go to the marches. The gay rednecks would rather be caught dead."

The closet also remains an issue among Nashville's African-American gay men and lesbians. Hardin is distressed by the

small turnout of black people to Pride and other gay and lesbian events. "I've done everything to get the black folks to
come out," she says. "There's a lot of fear. They feel like they're
not going to have a chance, that their families will reject them.
And it happens. I've seen blacks kill themselves after their families found out. Most black gays here live double lives. There is
one black gay club, the Highway, and it is packed wall to wall
black with folks—three hundred, four hundred people—so I
know our numbers are strong. But that place is about as public
as they go, and a lot won't even go there."

Hardin feels that if she and her "wife" can be out as African-
American lesbians—and raise a child—"anyone can," and that's
her message to other black gay men and lesbians. "I've lived
with a black woman for nine years," she tells me. "She's from a
small city, Smithville, Tennessee. She was the only openly gay
person there, and her people were the only black people up
there. When we got together, I said, 'I'm not closeted. I've never
worn a dress and I'm not dying to wear one now.' I told her I'm
very political about being openly gay. And she said, 'Well that's
the only way, then.'

"We have a thirteen-year-old son—he's her son by a previous marriage—and one thing we make clear with the
teachers at school is that we're lesbians and they have to
make sure that that baby gets an education. He goes to a predominantly all-black school, and they're fine with it, and he
deals with it."

Hardin's dream is to move into the country, where she says a
lot of gay men and lesbians now live. "I've got one friend who's
got two hundred acres, and she wouldn't be anywhere else," she
says. "Another one has a horse farm, eighty acres of land. She
raises horses and dogs. They're living wonderful lives. Yes, I
would love to buy me about eighty acres of land and just move

up there and live there and live with my family and seven horses. It all has to do with what you're willing to accept and what you're comfortable with," Hardin says of her choice. "Look at Chicago. It's big. If you're gay, it's more open and accepting of you. You can ride the rails and hold hands with your lover while doing so. That's great. But you can't find grass and cows and a barnyard to go in and sit and talk.

"Years ago, you had to move away from here. Even today, a lot of the country people come out and go to the big cities; they go to where the gay clan is. But after they've lived the life for a while and learned the truth, they can go back to where they started because they can deal with it. That's what it comes down to for a lot of us: getting enough knowledge to deal with the situation, and coming back home."

Out, **September 1997**

BAREBACK AND RECKLESS

"ARE YOU POSITIVE OR negative?" I ask the handsome twenty-seven-year-old on America Online. He's just sent me his GIF—photo—and it's true to his online profile: six-foot, 180, "good-looking Italian" with a lean, muscular body. His profile adds that he's a bottom who likes going at it "for hours," that he's into "bareback sex," and that prospective sexual partners had better "ask what that is first." Also known as "skin-to-skin" or "raw," among several other terms, "going bareback" quite simply means having anal sex without condoms.

"Not sure about my status," he types back at me.

"Do you figure you're probably poz?" I ask.

"Well, last I checked it was neg, but not sure 'cause I like taking it raw and have done so a lot," he replies.

"Do you have any concern about becoming poz?"

"I have a concern about it, sure. But love it raw, even with that concern."

"Pete" explains to me how he sets up potential dates, making sure that guys are into having sex without condoms. "I don't ask about guys' HIV status normally," he says. "I'd rather not know 'cause it only adds more stress." He says that he generally doesn't allow them to ejaculate inside of him—"but it some-times happens"—and that he doesn't usually swallow semen during oral sex except if he's "really into" the guy.

"What if you become positive?" I ask. "Is it worth it?"

"Well, I'd like to stay neg," he tells me. "But it's a very manageable disease with the meds today. I'd probably not die from it."

"The thing about the drugs," I say, referring to protease inhibitors, the class of drugs misguidedly touted by some as a near-cure for HIV, "is that I've got positive friends who are already crashing—the drugs worked for a little while, but now they don't. They also often have horrible side effects—violent diarrhea, stuff like that. Also, no one knows how long the drugs will inhibit HIV, or how toxic they'll be in the long run. And it's an unbelievable regimen, sometimes twenty pills a day."

"It *is* a big deal," he replies. "But it's manageable."

We meet for coffee. Pete is warm and personable and looks every bit like his photo: muscular and sexy. He has sex mostly with guys he meets online and out in the clubs, he says, and the thrill of going bareback makes the sex hotter. Pete also goes to all the big dance events, the "circuit" parties. "Love partying with crystal [methamphetamine] and Ecstasy," he tells me, recounting a night out at a recent circuit event in New York. "It was a blast—that night I went home and got fucked by my ex-roommate for two hours, raw."

It would be comforting to just say that Pete is one of the very few gay men who at this point are still "uneducated" about AIDS. Most people know, after all, that pre-come has extremely high concentrations of HIV, right? Doesn't everyone also know that protease inhibitors are no picnic? And everyone must realize that safer sex is more important than ever, with the possibility of a drug-resistant strain of super-HIV developing. But no, the most shocking thing that Pete tells me is when I ask him what kind of work he does. "I'm in the health-care industry," he says.

Pete is one of two dozen men I've interviewed who either say they are negative or are unsure of their status—many of them professional, educated men—who have decided to forgo condoms; he is, in fact, one of more than 250 users who have the word "bareback" in their America Online profiles. If this sudden prevalence in cyberspace is any indication, these men are just the tip of a larger, dangerous iceberg. Their behavior, which seems to have been greatly influenced by the advent of protease inhibitors, could have a devastating effect on efforts to contain the AIDS epidemic, and ultimately on the entire lesbian and gay community.

Going bareback is nothing new. It's a choice HIV-positive men have faced for years. Although some medical professionals warn of "reinfection" with other strains of HIV, and of other sexually transmitted diseases, some choose to forgo condoms when they are the anal receptive partner or when having any kind of sex with other HIV-positive men.

It's impossible to know, however, how widespread the practice of premeditated unprotected sex, for the sheer thrill of it, is among men who engage in anonymous multiple-partner sex—men who last tested negative or have never been tested. Bareback chat rooms have sprung up all over the Internet, and bareback sex parties are now quite common, where negative may mix with positive. *Poz* magazine, which sometimes seems to eerily glamorize AIDS, even ran a piece recently extolling the joys of bareback sex (the HIV-positive writer said he "can't comment" on negative men barebacking). Some gay men believe that if protease inhibitors reduce viral load to undetectable levels, there's no reason to worry about infection or reinfection—though no studies back this up.

Most HIV-prevention efforts in recent years have focused on men who are "slipping up" in the heat of passion or while on drugs or alcohol, and, to a lesser extent, on men who fall in love and decide to go without condoms with their partner. The idea that fast-lane HIV-negative men like Pete might consciously decide to give up condoms seems to have been, well, unthinkable—particularly before protease inhibitors. But it's clearly a growing, alarming phenomenon.

Even more frightening is a parallel new trend toward eroticizing the virus, where men actually talk about desiring both to infect others (if they are positive) or to become infected (if they are negative). One HIV-positive man I talked to, a proctologist from the Midwest, told me that he'd love to give me "the gift," meaning HIV. Under a pseudonym, I had told him that I was negative but tired of using condoms. "That's just it," he said. "You don't have to use them any longer. With the new drugs, being HIV positive is not a major problem any more. It's a miracle. That's why, at this point, HIV is a gift."

On a Web site called XtremeSex, gay men in fact talk of "gift-giving" and of receiving "that hot poz load." Some men lament their difficulties in getting infected: "Guess I haven't gotten the right virulent strain yet." Recalling one bareback sex party, where negative and positive men came together without revealing their status, one formerly HIV-negative man recounted how he tested positive two weeks later. At home with his boyfriend, he writes, "one thing led to another. We fucked some, talked some. 'So are you infecting me?' he asked, real quiet. 'Yeah, I am.' "

John McCoy, a gay reporter for the *Dallas Voice,* wrote a piece about the Web site last April, and interviewed the man who founded it, who goes only by the screen name PigBotm. PigBotm told McCoy that he knew of men who threw a party when they seroconverted. Gary Shelden, a forty-five-year-old computer programmer from San Francisco, whom McCoy describes as a "willing HIV convert," told McCoy that he intentionally ignored safer-sex precautions with men he knew to be HIV positive. "I was certainly not accustomed to having safe sex," said Shelden, who had just come out of a sixteen-year monogamous relationship in which he did not use condoms. "I found that being HIV negative was standing in the way of my sex life, and my sex life is very important to me." Shelden got on protease inhibitors, paid for by private insurance, got his viral load down, and told McCoy that HIV "hasn't had a noticeable effect on my life."

Like quite a few of the bareback men I have interviewed and chatted with, Shelden and PigBotm spoke of HIV infection as now being a minor inconvenience. Similarly, McCoy found the bareback men had a disdain for AIDS-prevention advocates and for the government, deeming as sex-negative "traitors" those who criticized their behavior.

"Our sex lives are not dispensable," a Washington, D.C., man told me, defending bareback sex. He's still HIV negative, he says, and gets tested every six months. His plan should he seroconvert is to get on protease inhibitors right away. "It's homophobic for you to tell me that I should not put my sex—my homosex—as a top priority in my life. Heterosexuals take similar risks in order to have babies. A lot of women are told by their doctors, for example, that, for whatever reason, it's too risky for them to have a baby. But they have it anyway. That is considered a justifiable reason to take a risk, but this is not. To me, that's just homophobia."

As bareback sex becomes more popular, the list of rationalizations offered by gay men longing for condom-free sex will continue to grow. But as we have seen, and as Gabriel Rotello shows so clearly in his book, *Sexual Ecology* (Dutton), it only takes a core group of people having multiple-partner unsafe sex to keep seroprevalence in the greater gay community high enough for the epidemic to continue unabated. We are now faced with perhaps the most challenging and frightening questions that the AIDS epidemic has ever raised: Will we be able to sustain wave after wave of HIV infection? What if protease inhibitors go the way of AZT and begin to fizzle out? How will we continue to get hard-fought funding from the government, and compassion from our liberal friends, when they learn that a small but growing group of people within our own community are behaving recklessly and selfishly? How can many lesbians and a great many gay men themselves not throw their hands in the air, rightly disgusted and anguished?

Perhaps most important, what do HIV-prevention leaders do now? Having found it difficult enough to grapple with men who are "slipping up," now they have to come to terms with what could be a significant number of people who are willfully and sometimes angrily defying safer-sex efforts, rebelling against the rest of us, and thereby keeping HIV transmission thriving, affecting adversely the entire gay world.

The answers are far from easy, but this much is clear: What looked like a bright and glorious future, an end to the epidemic, could easily turn into a disaster for us all, one worse than what we have seen so far. Over fifteen years ago, when AIDS first surfaced, many of us stuck our heads in the sand and—along with the government and the media—allowed the situation to get out of control. Will we not learn from our own past?

Out, **July 1997**

Note: Being among the first to write about the "bareback" phenomenon in 1997 is a distinction I could have lived without, particularly if it we could turn everything back to where an increase in unsafe sex was not plaguing the gay community. I was ridiculed and attacked for "Bareback and Reckless" when it was published in Out *in 1997, by some who did not want to face up to reality. The general charge: It was overblown and sensationalized. Looking back, however, it's painfully clear that this piece reflected only the tip of the iceberg, as unprotected sex among gay and bisexual men has grown dramatically, along with the complacency charted by two later pieces included in this collection.*

641,086 AND COUNTING

"It's lily-livered and ass-covering," Larry Kramer recently told me on the telephone in his usual blunt and passionate way. He was talking about an op-ed piece in the *New York Times* in June written by Dr. David Ho, *Time* magazine's 1996 Man of the Year and the scientist who pioneered protease inhibitors and cocktail therapies using combinations of several powerful drugs to fight AIDS. "He's a decent man, and he's also a smart man," Kramer continued. "I don't think we should crucify him too much, but I think the pathway that he and his minions have lead us down is at the moment troubling and uncertain."

Clearly written to defend against critics who have pointed to problems with the new drugs, Ho's piece attacked "scientists and commentators" who "offer a doomsday scenario, wherein patients on combination therapy deteriorate . . . because of the emergence of viral strains that are resistant to the drugs." The naysayers, Ho charged, put forth "alarming forecasts" and "exaggerated portrayals."

Well, call me Mr. Doomsday, Chicken Little, the Queer Who Cried Wolf, or whatever other name you can come up with. Because I now believe this with every fiber and bone in my body: Unless we break from the rampant apathy, selfishness, and denial that has landed on this community like an otherworldly invasion, we are headed toward an unqualified disaster—if we're not there already. A disaster in which protease inhibitors turn out not to be the cure-all they've been hyped to be by people and groups as diverse as the pharmaceutical industry, the media, Andrew Sullivan, sex guru Dan Savage, and Magic Johnson. A disaster in which safer-sex practices among gay men continue to diminish, in part due to that hype, as many gay men blindly believe the drugs make AIDS "manageable" and that it's not so bad to get HIV. A disaster in which drug-resistant strains of HIV—mutations of the virus bred in the bodies of some people with HIV in response to the drug therapy—begin spreading rapidly. A disaster in which our now-downsized AIDS-service organizations, as well as private and public health-care facilities that have cut back services because their AIDS caseloads dropped, become overwhelmed with very sick people. A disaster in which a new generation of gay men becomes as immersed in the horrors of disease and death as the previous generations.

In other words, I predict a replay of what happened over fifteen years ago when AIDS first surfaced. And people like David Ho, rather than leading the charge against this, are doing exactly what they did in the early 1980s: shoring up their reputations and continuing with business as usual, allowing drug companies and small cadres of individuals to dictate treatment—in this case, pursuing protease inhibitors like the Gold Rush—while they try to silence dissenters.

If we allow this to happen, we will have only ourselves to blame in the end. We allow it to happen by diverting our attention and time to peripheral and meaningless issues or plunging ourselves into our social worlds, our travels, and all the other escapist activities that a booming economy makes easy. We allow it to happen by becoming apolitical and complacent, smugly telling ourselves we're "post-AIDS" or "post-gay"—two terms du jour—turning denial into the latest fashion statement and a delectable sound bite. And we allow it to happen by following the seductive ideas of people whose message we so much want to believe: that AIDS is over.

In the case of David Ho, there's no question that he is a brilliant scientist who brought us the most important breakthrough in the seventeen years of the epidemic. Because of protease inhibitors, in the past two years thousands of people with HIV have risen from their deathbeds and are leading normal lives, and for that we should be immensely thankful. But spinning headily in his PR whirl, Ho made a dangerous claim that more and more scientists now see as a pipe dream: that protease inhibitors would eradicate HIV from the body. In a report published last spring, for example, Dr. William Paul, former director of the Office of AIDS Research at the National Institutes of Health, along with Tel Aviv University's Zvi Grossman, and Mark Feinberg of the National Institute of Allergy and Infectious Diseases, concluded in their own extensive research that HIV remains hidden in certain cells of the body even when it is not detectable in the blood, and that some virus-producing cells can survive more than two decades. Given the toxicity of protease inhibitors, they noted, it's doubtful most people can stay on the drugs more than a few years, making the drugs far from "curative."

Already, within the past two years, reports have emerged about often grotesque physical side effects of the drugs—in addition to the usual nausea, diarrhea, and other ailments associated with them—as well as about the failure of the drugs to continue to suppress HIV over a period of time. This has played out dramatically in my own life in the past year, as several HIV-positive friends who were fit and healthy thanks to the drugs suddenly began developing gaunt faces, hunchbacks, bizarre potbellies, strange fat deposits, and dangerously soaring cholesterol levels. And while I've had friends for whom the drugs didn't work from the get-go—mostly people who'd tried AZT and other drugs in the past and had thus built up a resistance to treatments—I've recently begun hearing unsettling scenarios from several who'd initially responded well to protease inhibitors. Their previously undetectable viral load is shooting back up—and often their T cells are dropping again as well. The virus is apparently developing resistance to the drugs and perhaps mutating itself into a super HIV inside their bodies.

Confirming these anecdotal reports, scientists at the World AIDS Conference in Geneva in June soberly presented studies that showed that anywhere from 15 percent to 60 percent of people on protease inhibitors are experiencing the deformative side effects. Considering that these powerful and toxic drugs have not been in wide usage for more than two years, it's not alarmist to think that these side effects might eventually affect everyone taking the drugs, and that new and more deadly side effects may emerge in time. Researchers in Geneva also presented data that showed that 30 percent to 50 percent of those on protease inhibitors are developing resistance to the drugs. A

Stanford University study published last spring of 200 San Francisco Bay Area people with AIDS on protease inhibitors found that half are partially resistant to the drugs and 20 percent don't respond to the drugs at all. Again, because of the relatively short time people have been taking these drugs, it's fair to speculate the worst—that everyone on the drugs might eventually develop resistance.

Couple this information with the just-published Seropositive Urban Gay Men's Study of HIV-positive men in New York and San Francisco, in which 22 percent reported that in the previous three months they had engaged in unprotected insertive anal sex with partners who were HIV negative or whose HIV status was unknown. Throw in the news from Geneva that the much-hyped idea of an AIDS vaccine now looks far less promising than it had and the observations of many researchers who speculate that the "bareback" craze is in part due to some gay men believing AIDS to be not so deadly any longer. And then add to the mix perhaps the most lethal ingredient: the *New England Journal of Medicine* report this summer of the first documented case of transmission of a protease-resistant strain of HIV. The infected San Francisco man says he was exposed to the virus after one episode of unprotected receptive anal sex that did not even reach the point of ejaculation, with a man who'd developed resistance to the drugs. Similarly, one of the romantic bards of barebacking, Sex Panic! activist Stephen Gendin, says he has transmitted his drug-resistant strain to his previously HIV-negative partner. (Gendin now reports feeling "guilty and confused.") Studies from Switzerland and San Francisco show that roughly one out of thirty new HIV infections is of a drug-resistant strain. What we have here is a recipe for disaster—a cocktail more potent than even the most toxic combination therapy.

"It's like you were time-warped back to 1983, when there were no drugs at all," commented Anthony S. Fauci, director of the National Institute of Allergy and Infectious Diseases, of the scary phenomenon of transmission of drug-resistant strains. He may as well have been talking about the political and psychological time warp we're all in, as we play out an old script from the early 1980s.

Just as in 1983, drug companies, fueled by the usual corporate greed, are ignoring people's needs, while we remain silent. With our AIDS activism at an all-time low, the industry is pursuing treatment based on what they perceive to be a "sure thing" rather than spending money researching and pursuing every possible avenue. It's true that companies are vigorously developing more effective protease inhibitors that involve less-complicated regimens and which may cut down on side effects. But as Martin Delaney, director of the San Francisco–based AIDS advocacy group Project Inform, has said, "We need more than just better versions of what we already have—we need whole new approaches to treatment."

As in 1983, we also are staying silent while the federal government refuses to fund the most crucial forms of HIV prevention: broad-based condom-education and needle-exchange programs. And as in 1983, we are staying silent while many of our own people, in pathetic and offensive displays of self-absorption, tell us AIDS is not a big deal and that we should stop thinking about it as a "crisis."

In his famous "End of AIDS" piece in the *New York Times Magazine* in 1996, Andrew Sullivan told us that, since the drugs are working for him, AIDS is over, and that it is we who are the ones in denial. (Earth to Andrew: Come in, please.) The hip sex-advice columnist Dan Savage, whose work I've always loved, soon thereafter wrote a widely syndicated article stating that since he was negative and since he was in a monogamous relationship—and since Andrew Sullivan had now said it was OK—he was no longer seeing AIDS as something about which he needed to concern himself, and that he was in fact sick of hearing about it. In the *Village Voice,* the article was proudly head-lined "The AIDS Crisis Is Over—for Me."

Is it just me, or does this strike you as nothing but grade-A, middle-class yuppie egotism and self-indulgence? In the early 1990s, one of our chants at ACT UP demonstrations, directed at both homosexuals and heterosexuals, was, "We're fighting for your lives too!" Yes, it was about AIDS, but it was also about health care and greed, about how things were done in this country, and about how we had to change it for everyone—and we *did* change the drug-approval process, not just for AIDS drugs, but for drugs for cancer, Alzheimer's, and other illnesses as well. We cared about each other, and we cared about others. Why is bald-faced selfishness now posited as some radical and hip new idea?

It's perhaps not surprising to learn that Savage blurbed one of the nuttiest books about the epidemic to emerge this year, Eric Rofes's *Dry Bones Breathe* (Harrington Park Press). While the book has received hardly any attention, and the few reviews I've read were quite critical of Rofes's wacky-yet-dangerous premise, I mention it here as an illustration of how even some of our brightest people can sink to the depths of AIDS denial. Rofes was once a sane voice in HIV prevention, a former exec-utive director of San Francisco's Shanti Project and Los Angeles's Gay and Lesbian Center. The book posits that we are "post-AIDS" and have to start thinking that way. A longtime sex radical, Rofes can't seem to bear the idea that, in order to end the epidemic, gay sexual culture must go through some major changes. So he's decided we must simply accept the amount of HIV infection that we are experiencing and stop viewing AIDS as a "crisis." In other words, get used to it. Ignoring and distorting studies, Rofes, too, tells us that protease inhibitors are saving the day and that people should go on and lead their sex lives to their fullest, end of story.

It's odd that Eric Rofes, a longtime leftist activist, and Andrew Sullivan, known for his conservative views on gay issues as well as on affirmative action and feminism, would be in the same camp. But that's how AIDS denial works. It knows no political ideologies—it knows only the will to run away from reality, to forget the pain and the madness, to convince us that all is well and good. In the case of David Ho, a smart and well-meaning man, it's fueled by his desire to defend his positions to date and his role in getting us to this place. For Andrew Sullivan, it's about proving to the world—and to himself—that all is under control and that his life (and thus everyone else's) will be fine and normal. For Dan Savage, it's about closing himself off in his relationship and pretending AIDS does not exist. And for Eric Rofes, like many who don't want to face prevention realities for similar reasons, it's about protecting gay sexual culture as it now exists, at all costs.

Fueling post-AIDS rhetoric is its sister, the "post-gay" movement, an inchoate group of people and ideas that to me too often sounds like a fancy name for being apolitical and apathetic—not much different from post-AIDS. I'm all for getting beyond the trappings of the ghetto—the superficial party scene, the drugs, the body fascism, the conformity in thought and values—but that doesn't mean being disengaged from activism and denying the struggle we are experiencing in this country. As long as the religious right is breathing down our necks, seizing political power and labeling us the enemy, we don't have the luxury of being post-gay. We will never be post-gay while senators are condemning us in Congress. We will never be post-gay while thugs are seeking us out, on the city streets as well as far beyond the cities, to bash our skulls in. We will never be post-AIDS while states as supposedly liberal as New York pass laws mandating name collection of those who test HIV positive, despite the fact that New York City is a place the post-gay crowd says is now safe and free from prejudice (wait until their names get on a list). Post-gay theorizing is also part of the early 1980s time warp. It harkens back to a complacent time when many gay people believed that they'd been accepted in American society, that Stonewall and the activism of the 1970s had earned them visibility and respect in the culture simply because they could boogie on a dance floor all night without fear of the club being raided. Then AIDS came along, bringing to the surface the governmental indifference, homophobia, and hatred that had always been there, underscoring that we had few rights at all.

Yes, it's true that there is one key element that distinguishes this moment in the epidemic from the early '80s: People are not dying in the same numbers. Death rates due to AIDS in the gay male community have plunged, thanks to the drugs. But HIV transmission has not stopped, and seroprevalence rates are still too high. What happens when more and more gay men on protease inhibitors succumb to the disfiguring side effects or when new side effects develop? What happens when the drugs stop working for many or all? What happens when the drug-resistant strains continue spreading? Will it take massive death and suffering for us to wake up once again? Back in 1983, Larry Kramer had already spent two years running from bar to bar in New York, giving speeches at rallies, and writing blistering missives in the *New York Native,* warning people about a plague that was emerging. Most people thought he was a crank. "Somehow

there are waves of rumor that the epidemic is waning, that figures have slowed down, that, as in some fairy tale, we're all on
our way to a happy ending and we can return to apathy and
closetry," he wrote in the article "2,339 and Counting" in the
Village Voice in October of that year. "How can we be so dumb
and blind and ignorant?. . . How can anyone believe things are
getting better?" Indeed, things only got far, far worse.

Out, **September 1998**

MURDER AMONG THE RUINS

THE ODOR IN THE stairwell had become too much to bear, and it seemed to emanate from under one particular door. So on the morning of August 9, 1997, Fabio Capri, the landlord of the building, summoned the carabinieri—the Italian police—who soon entered the elegant apartment on Via Pio Foa in the Monteverde section of Rome, a space decorated with expensive furnishings and artworks from Japan and the Orient. There, in the dining room, lying facedown, was the badly decomposed body of Louis Inturissi, the man who'd been so proud of his balcony, overflowing with rare flowers and plants watered by an elaborate sprinkler system.

He had been dead for four days or longer, and his body was

almost naked, his pants pulled down to his ankles. The apartment bore no sign of forced entry, and half-full wineglasses were sitting on the table alongside an open bottle of wine. The fifty-six-year-old Connecticut-born American writer, *New York Times* contributor, and university professor, who'd taught English at Rome's John Cabot University, had apparently been hit several times over the head with a blunt object. The apartment had been ransacked, but all that was missing was Inturissi's wallet, with some cash.

Six weeks after the murder, when I traveled around Italy to look into this and a number of other, similar killings, Inturissi's friends weighed in on this vivacious, well-mannered gentleman with exquisite taste. "He was very much a part of the *New York Times* family here," says Celestine Bohlen, the Rome bureau chief of the *Times*. "He was a man with an enormous knowledge of Italy, an astute observer of the Italian people."

"We were charmed by him," the novelist David Leavitt tells me with fondness, as he and I and his partner, Mark Mitchell, chat at the dining-room table of their apartment in Rome, half a block from the Coliseum. "He was an extremely exuberant, funny, witty man."

While it appeared that Inturissi had allowed his murderer into his home, and perhaps had just engaged in sex with him, Leavitt and other friends say that Inturissi had never mentioned dating anyone. In fact, he put forth the idea that he rarely engaged in sex at all. "He used to say, 'I'm a monk,' " Leavitt recalls with a smile, leaning over the sleek glass table. The only times that Inturissi even broached the subject of sex, Leavitt says, was once when Inturissi and another friend discussed an underground male-prostitution service in Rome they'd heard tales about, and another time when Inturissi revealed his knowledge of a particular cruising area where young male prostitutes often plied their trade. "He said that his only interest in going there was to get [rare plant] cuttings," Leavitt recalls.

But gay activists and gay journalists in Italy believe that Inturissi was killed by a young hustler whom he'd hired for sex. "The police have told me that they haven't gotten really concrete evidence because the body was badly decomposed and there is therefore no forensic evidence," Andrea Pini, a dark-haired Roman schoolteacher and journalist who has investigated the murder for the Italian gay magazine *Babilonia,* tells me as we stroll across the Piazza Navona, a nighttime hangout for many of Rome's young people. "And while they have not yet made a public statement, they have told me that from the evidence they have it bears all the markings of a crime that involved gay prostitution. And I agree."

Pini is so sure about this because he has studied quite a few remarkably similar murders in recent years. The murder of Louis Inturissi fits into a pattern of murders of older men known or thought to be gay or bisexual and often believed to frequent male hustlers—Pini counts at least nineteen such murders in Rome alone since 1990. And Franco Grillini, president of Arcigay, Italy's national gay organization, estimates that nationwide, for the past ten years or more, there have been over 100 such murders—per year.

It was only eight months prior to Inturissi's murder, in January 1997, when the upper crust of Florence was rocked by the slaying of Count Alvise di Robilant, a Florentine aristocrat and art collector who was the director of Sotheby's Italia. The seventy-two-year-old divorced father of three was bludgeoned in his magnificent third-century-A.D. apartment. His naked body was found on the floor, and he, too, had been hit over the head several times with a blunt object. There was no evidence of forced entry; di Robilant and his murderer appeared to have been drinking champagne just prior to the killing. Nothing in the apartment filled with priceless original artworks was stolen—though di Robilant's favorite painting, which hung over his bed, had been slashed violently.

Perhaps because di Robilant had a reputation as a septuagenarian jet-set playboy, the media and the police did not initially hypothesize that that his killer might have been a male hustler. But three months later, the autopsy reported that di Robilant had the fresh sperm of another man in his mouth at the time of his death.

"At first, some did not believe the hypothesis of a gay murder because of the many relations Alvise had with different women," reported *La Repubblica.* "But the biological liquid revealed what happened during the last minutes of Alvise's life."

While the killings of di Robilant and Inturissi received national coverage, scores of other murders over the past several years of men known or thought to be gay have received little attention at all. Throughout the ten days I spent in Italy, I heard of dozens of such killings: In Rome, a forty-nine-year-old hair-stylist, Claudio Pavoni, was killed in his apartment, beaten with an ashtray and lamps; a fifty-year-old theater critic, Dante Cappelletti, was strangled in his apartment with a telephone cord; and Mario Chiarani, a sixty-seven-year-old retired hotel owner, was tied up nude and suffocated with a cloth stuffed in his mouth. In the Adriatic resort city of Rimini, a thirty-eight-year-old municipal clerk was stabbed in his home while in female drag. A thirty-four-year-old designer who lived in the town of Ronco dell'Adige in the north was bludgeoned, tied up with electrical cord, and thrown into the Adige River. In Naples, a forty-year-old architect was found with his skull bashed in and with his pants down in an area frequented by male prostitutes. The list goes on and on: a sixty-year-old actor, a fifty-four-year-old hotel manager, a fifty-three-year-old priest, a thirty-seven-year-old engineer, a fifty-four-year-old tarot-card reader.

While these murders date back at least as far as 1990, it was not until after the murders of di Robilant and Inturissi that the media began to focus on the larger pattern. By August 20, the Milan newspaper, *Corriere della Sera,* threw out the term "Cunanan Romano"—Rome's Cunanan—as the Inturissi murder occurred shortly after the star-studded memorial service in Milan for the Italian designer Gianni Versace, slain by Andrew Cunanan, a onetime prostitute, in Miami's South Beach. But in fact, no evidence points to a single psychopathic serial killer. Perhaps more frightening, the slayings are apparently being carried out by many desperate young men.

"I'd like to go London, to look for work, or attend photography school, and the ultimate place would be New York—that is my dream," eighteen-year-old Alessandro tells me, as we sit in the rustic, book-laden Rome apartment of the university professor with whom he has been staying. The boy is tall and lanky with big brown eyes, a dastardly smile, and the raw scent of a boy who has not bathed in a couple of days. A hustler who has been working the parks and piazzas of Rome for only a couple of months now, Alessandro is originally from a small town on the island of Sardinia, in the Mediterranean, where his father worked in the mines. He came to Rome with a job lined up working for the city, but it fell through within weeks of his arrival. He met some young friends, other boys, who introduced him to hustling. They meet men at parks like the Monte Caprino or Villa Borghese, or in gay nightclubs that cater to hustlers and their johns, such as Incognito 2000.

Like just about every male hustler in Rome, Alessandro says he is strictly heterosexual and does not like the work he is doing. But, he says, it's good money that he can't turn down. Indeed, there seems to be no equivalent to the middle-class, gay-identified West Hollywood bodybuilders with beepers who sell themselves by the hour and make house calls, or to the large and established escort services offering buff gay men in splashy advertisements in dozens of stateside gay publications. Most hustlers I see working the parks and streets of Rome, Milan, Florence, and elsewhere are either straight-identified and boyish or they are transvestites and transsexuals. And they are for the most part poor and working the streets. And until recently, several gay activists explain, they were almost all Italian, like Alessandro, from the poorer South or from the islands of Sicily and Sardinia. But in recent years Italy has been hit by a wave of immigration, and a great many of the young male hustlers today are from Romania, Albania, Poland, and North Africa.

"They're coming from cultures that are very homophobic, violently so," says Andrea Pini. "The police have said that most of the killings, they believe, are being carried out by Romanian men. Romania is very antigay. Homosexuality is punishable by law. So they have an extremely low regard for homosexuals."

Yet the murders do not appear premeditated—the weapon is usually something in the home, and often little is stolen. Something just seems to make the men snap. Perhaps the client catches the hustler in an act of theft, Pini speculates, or "perhaps the client wants to do something that wasn't agreed to, and it insults the hustler." Pini is alluding to the motive put forth by the male hustler who murdered the famed Italian film director Pier Paolo Pasolini in 1975; the murderer, whom Pini has interviewed in prison, claimed that Pasolini was trying to anally penetrate him against his wishes.

"For some of the men," Pini says, "just the suggestion that they take the passive role is a threat to their masculinity and would certainly arouse anger."

In other cases, Pini and others observe, S/M sex play may get out of hand. Alessandro tells me about an experience he had: "I had one man who wanted me to beat him up and who couldn't have an orgasm unless I beat him," he says, batting his long, dark eyelashes and launching into a chilling tale. "He was very, very happy to have me beat him. He picked me up in Rome but took me up to Florence, to his house. He kept saying 'Hit me! Hit me in the face! Hit me in the head!' So I did. He then had me also beat him with a club, again and again. He was bleeding, but still saying, 'Hit me! Pick me up and throw me against the wall!' The funny thing was that, after he had the orgasm, he wanted me to keep going and told me to kick him. He was on the floor in a ball, and I was just kicking him and kicking him. You don't understand why they like this kind of perversion, but you just collaborate with it." He cracks a smile. "And you know, I enjoyed it." Arcigay president Grillini believes that some people are scapegoating the foreign hustlers just a little too much. Having been active in gay politics in Italy for the past twenty years, he does not believe there is necessarily an increase in the number of such murders in recent years but that they are only getting more attention today because homosexuality itself is more in the news. "Years ago, you'd read about or hear about similar murders: an older guy found tied up or killed in his house," he says, sitting at his desk in Arcigay's charming Bologna offices, housed in a decayed piece of the old wall that surrounded the city. "And we might know he was gay and figure it out, but nobody else would—not the media or the police, certainly."

One reason hustler-related murders might be so prevalent— and why they might always have been so prevalent—is simply that gay male prostitution itself is somewhat of a grand tradition in Italy. And that, say many gay Italians, is because the average gay Italian man you meet in a bar is not "out" in the American sense of the word. Young people, those in their twenties and thirties, who might even identify to each other as *gay* or *lesbica*, more often than not are still living with their families, who don't know of their sexual orientation, and many older men who engage in homosexual sex are married to women. Most of the reported murders have been of married men or men who were single but very secretive about their sexual behavior. It's all part of the paradox of homosexuality in Italy: While neither outlawed nor railed against by right-wingers, gay sex remains largely undiscussed and underground, however widespread. The stage for these ongoing murders was in fact set hundreds of years ago, when the social institutions that still grip Italy established this country's particular way of dealing with its citizens' sexual activities.

It is Friday night at 11:00 in Milan, and Ricci, an elegant pasticceria—bakery and café—in the Piazza della Repubblica is packed. Exquisitely dressed, statuesque men with chiseled jaws chat in small groups, occasionally locking eyes with a passing male stranger. Most of the women here, sleek and slim, are on one side of the room. "Ricci attracts *à la page* lesbians," tall, handsome Giuseppe Andrisani tells me, using a French term to describe the chic women. One of Milan's oldest and most respected pasticcerias, Ricci becomes a trendy gay club on Friday nights, and this night, the crowd is overflowing onto the sidewalk. It is Fashion Week, and people have jetted in from around the world.

This is one of the reasons Andrisani prefers Milan to the rest of Italy; it is more worldly and sophisticated, he says. But even

Milan remains part of the paradox of gay life in this Mediterranean country. "I don't feel there is intense homophobia in the culture," says Andrisani, a thirty-one-year-old dentist, the following afternoon as we chat over cocktails in the ornate lobby of the Hotel Diana Majestic. "There are not laws against you, like in the States. But still, it is not okay the way things are here, because gays are not considered normal. We are just not visible." I point out to him that part of that invisibility is surely due to the fact that at age thirty-one he has still not told his family about his sexual orientation—which is clearly the norm for gay men and lesbians of all ages in Italy. He cracks a smile. "Yes, I know," he says. "But my family would be upset, and I love them too much. My mother goes to church almost every day. I know she must know about me, but she wouldn't want to hear me say it."

Andrisani articulates the central contradiction of being gay in Italy, a sentiment that many people express to me as I travel the country over several weeks investigating these ongoing murders. What has set the stage for this horror, I've found, is in part the incongruity that Andrisani and others represent: People profess to accept homosexuality—their own or someone else's—yet they want it kept it out of sight and out of mind.

Andrisani attended school in Manhattan, and lived and worked for two years in Los Angeles. "I like it better here," he explains, leaning back on the lobby's burgundy leather sofa, "because in L.A. I felt like I was stuck in a ghetto. You are very free to do whatever you like within the borderlines of West Hollywood. Everywhere else there is a lot of homophobia and the politicians are saying antigay things. Here I feel more free. Here we don't have these gay neighborhoods. Everything is mixed. In my building, there are two gays, and most of the neighbors, I think, know it. If you see two people holding hands, it's no big deal. Here," he continues, "there is no reason here to declare your homosexuality. What do you get from it?"

In the United States, the average informed lesbian or gay American could answer that question with a long list of reasons to be out, reasons that would have everything to do with fighting blatant discrimination and antigay hatred and physical violence. But in Italy, there are no Pat Buchanan–style political figures railing against lesbians and gay men, demanding that homophobia be written into law. There are no laws barring sexual contact between people of the same gender, and a person cannot be fired from his or her job or thrown out of his or her apartment simply for being gay or lesbian. And no one is ejected from the military simply for declaring their homosexuality.

In fact, a number of Italian cities have domestic-partnership benefits, granting couples deductions on rental units, and Italy's largest trade union also recently reached out to gay men and lesbians. Some Italian gay activists and journalists speculate that this Catholic country surrounding the Vatican could even legally recognize same-sex unions well before the United States. Italy has been especially ambitious about being a European Union member in good standing, and as the EU solidifies, the more progressive and gay-friendly Northern European countries— like Denmark and the Netherlands, where same-sex unions are recognized—are pressuring other member nations to adopt similar policies. "Even if people weren't supportive, it is conceivable Italy would recognize [same-sex unions]," says Giovanni Dall'-Orto, a prominent gay journalist and author. "The politicians [could] tell the voters that they had to do it in order to gain more acceptance in the EU, which people are very much in favor of."

The kinds of life-and-death issues that create fear and heartache among gay people in the United States—and therefore galvanize them to activism—don't have the same impact in

Italy. Most gay men and lesbians I meet, from Milan to Rome to Bologna, say they don't know anyone with AIDS, and U.S.-style gay-bashing seems to be relatively rare. "I don't ever hear of much of that, except occasionally with neo-Nazi skinhead violence," says Sarah Sajetti, editorial director of *Babilonia,* Italy's national gay magazine.

The strange catch-22 is that this largely nonthreatening atmosphere is likely a result of the absence of any public discussion of homosexuality. As Dall'Orto puts it, "You have to recognize something before you go beating up on it." And it's that invisibility—and the resulting underworld of hustlers and johns, coupled with a lack of press coverage and police insensitivity—that has, in part, allowed the murders to continue.

Heading from north to south in Italy, gay life becomes increasingly less visible, reflecting differences in the larger culture. Closest to the Northern European or American model is Milan, with fashionable places like Ricci and Elefante, frequented by gay men and lesbians, and big discos like Plastic, Pape Satan, and Pervert. There's After Line, where many working-class lesbians go, and No Ties and Nuova Idea, frequented by drag queens and transvestites. And there are gyms, nightclubs, bathhouses, several leather bars, even an *orsi* scene—"bears."

Farther south, the various camps begin to merge, and gay life is much more underground. In Florence, lesbian socializing is relegated to coffee shops and house parties, and the male baths, sparsely attended, close by 11:00 P.M. At the gay male bar Crisco, I had to become a "member" to enter. Once inside, I met several married men who were out for a few hours after dinner. Still farther south, in Naples, the scene is less about even discreet bars and baths and much more about furtive cruising on streets and in piazzas, and in the parks.

Rome is where northern and southern Italy converge. For a world-class city its size—with more than 2 million people—it has a shockingly small number of gay male bars, and almost no visible lesbian scene at all. Until recently, the chief activity for gay men was cruising the streets and piazzas and monuments. Prior to the installation of fences a few years ago, the hot cruising spot for outdoor sex was the Coliseum, and urban gay gossip has it that the bushes at the Circus Maximus were chopped down at the request of the Vatican because too many priests were getting arrested having sex there. More gay men are now meeting in the bars, but open-air cruising is far from expunged.

In many senses, Rome is experiencing a clash of two distinct male homosexual cultures: the newer, more public Northern European or American-influenced way, in which men define themselves as "gay" no matter what role they take in sex; and the Southern tradition, what Dall'Orto calls "Mediterranean homosexuality." In this older model, the "homosexual" is the one who engages in the passive role and is called a "ricchione" or, for those who cross-dress, a "femminella," while the active partner is the "normal" man, still considered heterosexual. It is a mostly underground culture reminiscent of an earlier, perhaps pre-industrial time.

Many of the hustlers who work the streets of Italian cities come from the South or from other countries with a more "Mediterranean" tradition and typically look down on—if not despise—their *ricchione* clientele. "The hustlers from North Africa and Albania are from violently antigay places," says Franco Grillini, president of Arcigay. "These are encounters where both the prostitute and the client are often doing something that they think is disturbing and shameful, terrible and ugly."

Indeed, for many of the older Italian men who patronize hustlers, "coming out" is a concept of a new gay world of which they are not a part. For them, getting married, leading heterosexual lives, and having homosexual sex on the side is the only paradigm they know. Meanwhile, the younger generation—those who may have embraced a gay or lesbian identity—are not doing much to teach them or the rest of Italy anything different, because they confine their "coming out" to select circles of friends and coworkers. And they feel no political pressure to do otherwise.

"There has been more progress in public opinion and in the general acceptance of homosexuality in Italy than there has been in the confidence of the homosexuals themselves to live their lives openly," Vanni Piccolo tells me as we stroll the streets of Rome on a warm late-autumn night. An animated, witty man, Piccolo is the adviser to Mayor Francesco Rutelli on gay issues. Rome's mayor has raised hackles at the Vatican by reaching out to gay men and lesbians and attending a Gay Pride parade. "We don't have the politicians of the kind that you have," Piccolo says, gesturing with his hands as we pause in front of a brightly lit café. "We don't have those people ranting and raving on the television. And one of the most notable changes in the past twenty years has been the attitude of people at the top in the police department. Why don't gays take advantage of it? Everything is in place for us to liberate ourselves. The people keeping gays back are gays themselves."

As politicians go, Rutelli, a member of the Democratic Party of the Left, is the exception, rather than the rule. Most politicians simply don't address the issue at all. To most Italian gay activists, the state is playing a cunning game, neither opposing gay rights nor granting them explicitly. Domestic-partnership

laws, for example, are worded so that any two people—two heterosexual friends, for example—could utilize them; same-sex
couples are not mentioned in the statutes. Similarly, statutes
forbid job discrimination on the basis of people's political or
philosophical beliefs; it's understood that sexual orientation is
included, but it's not listed explicitly. This kind of passive
progress is perhaps best exemplified by the Italian policy on
homosexuality in the military. A year of service is required of all
men at age eighteen, and a man cannot be exempted or ejected
for simply being gay, because the policy states that homosexuality cannot be considered a pathological condition. According
to Arcigay president Grillini, however, a gay man may exempt
himself for the "psychic suffering that accompanies" being gay,
due to homophobia in society. Grillini describes this policy as
the only privilege gay people enjoy in Italy—permission to
avoid "wasting a year of their lives."

"It's the culture—it's so powerful that the state doesn't need
to make laws against you," Nina Peci tells me. "It's a part of the
Catholic tradition, keeping your public life and your private life
separate. People don't want to join a 'gay movement.' Even in
the cities where they have [domestic-partnership laws], people
don't take advantage of them." Peci, a thirty-three-year-old
American who has lived in Italy for nine years, runs her own
advertising agency in Florence, where we are chatting in a
friend's scenic top-floor apartment one afternoon as church
bells ring throughout the city. An energetic, passionate woman
with short brown hair and a big smile, Peci is very involved in
local gay activism, and she publishes her own 'zine, *Quir.* "It's a
much better way for the state to keep you down," she says. "It's
very smart. If they make laws against you, or speak out against
you, then they call attention to you. And if they don't, you'll just
stay quiet."

The "culture" Peci refers to revolves around the institution of the family, which has a powerful grip over most people's lives—think of Giuseppe Andrisani's concern for his mother's feelings, or the many murdered patrons of male hustlers, who chose the closet in order to marry and have children. As Peci points out, it is a culture shaped by centuries of Catholic tradition, which dictates people's attitudes on sexual behavior in a much more powerful way than the state ever could.

As any Italian will tell you, most of Italy, is nothing like Northern Europe. "First of all," says Felice Mill Colorni, a writer who lives in the small city of Trieste, "we have no big city where gay people concentrate and where all kinds of people go, like London or Paris. There is a very strong tradition to stay in the city you were born in, and of course that is where your family is, so you don't go somewhere to experiment and live openly. Secondly, the welfare state is quite generous with the older people, but not with the younger people. This is one reason why Italians stay home much longer than in any other Western European society. The third thing is the Catholic heritage. But it is not, as foreigners think, because the Catholic teaching has a very strong power over actual sexual behavior. All of the statistics in fact show that people don't follow the Catholic Church. No, there is rather a way of life that is reinforced by Catholic tradition and the family structure."

Adds Giovanni Dall'Orto, "In Catholic countries, the thinking is, 'Do whatever you want, but just don't talk about.'" He smiles, referring not only to homosexuality but to married men who have female mistresses. "In Protestant countries, however, the thinking is, 'Talk about what you do—but just don't do it.' In fact, it's usually against the law. In most Protestant European countries and the United States there are, or were in the past, laws against homosexual activity. [And there,] the gay movement is more advanced. That is because in most Protestant countries the law defined 'the homosexual.' "

In Catholic countries like Spain, France, and Italy, Dall'Orto hypothesizes, the state has had no reason to make laws against homosexuality because the Catholic tradition so powerfully represses homosexuality on its own. The upside to this lack of political interference, Dall'Orto notes, is that gay people in these countries are not chained to the concept of sexual identity in the way Americans are, and often view it as a repressive pigeonholing of people. The downside, of course, is often an invisibility that serves the state in repressing homosexuality and instilling fear and terror in a lot of people. Of course, in a patriarchal country like Italy, many men continue to get away with gay sex on the side (though they risk the violence of trade or hustlers); women haven't even that option.

Vittoria Di Prizito moved to Rome a few months ago from Naples, where she grew up. She now lives with her partner and her partner's seventeen-year-old son. "My mother knows about me," she says. "She tries to understand. I think with lesbians in Italy, your mother will sometimes be more understanding because she understands the oppression of women and how difficult it is. My father only knows that I'm sharing a flat with a woman because I decided to look for a job in Rome."

Di Prizito tells me some harrowing stories: "When I was still living in Naples, I knew of two lesbians who were involved together, and one of them was kidnapped by her own family when they found out. They took her to a convent. Her girlfriend was desperately trying to find her, and the parents were telling her to go away. In the town of Ancona, a similar thing happened to another lesbian. And there are many women over forty who got married and had children and you meet them quite often in discos and in meeting places. They tell their husbands that they are going out with their friends, but they cannot do it so often."

The fear of being known keeps both lesbians and gay men from effective political organizing and has hindered efforts to bring police and public attention to the murders. Italy's gay organizations are tiny, and have little influence. Arcigay is run mostly by volunteers from a small office in Bologna. The group believes it cannot aggressively advocate that gay men and lesbians should "come out" and declare themselves.

"Gay people and lesbian people are forced into this situation," Franco Grillini explains. "The majority of gay men in Italy are married, with children. As a general rule, 90 percent of the Italian population lives in small towns [where] everyone wants to know everything about everyone, and social control is very strong. So, with the church and the family and this social pressure, we do understand that people cannot come out of the closet. We haven't got any gay community centers, where we can adopt people who are being thrown out of their houses. And they cannot live on their own."

Because so few people are involved politically, there is only one Gay Pride parade in all of Italy annually; it takes place in a different city each year and attracts activists and others from around the country. Last year, because of infighting, it was held in both Venice and Rome, and 2,000 people attended each event, out of a nation of 57 million. "There is no real gay movement," Sarah Sajetti, *Babilonia*'s editorial director, says bluntly. "Most of the activists themselves are even in the closet, and there's not a lot of organization." As if the movement weren't small enough, recently Italy's lesbian activists split off from Arcigay and formed a separate organization, Arcilesbica. "We want to foster the visibility of lesbians in Italy," says its president,

Titti De Simone, as she fields calls on her cell phone. "In a country like this, where gay is so invisible, lesbians are even less visible."

As always and everywhere, coming out is a long, uphill battle won in countless skirmishes often confined to families' living rooms. And each generation goes a bit further than the last. "The younger ones are now telling their parents, feeling they have to be honest, because there's more talk of it now," says Di Prizito. "A lot of teenagers are telling their parents, and even lesbians who are my age, late twenties, are doing it more so."

Yet most are probably coming out in a different way than in the States or Northern Europe, finding a uniquely Italian way to bring homosexuality home. "The new generation, they are starting to talk to their families about their sexuality when they are eighteen," says thirty-four-year-old Claudio Crisafi, a flight attendant based in Florence. We're sharing a pasta and tuna lunch that he has just cooked for us in his spacious, two-story apartment near the Duomo. "You will find a lot of people who are forty who will never tell their parents or their colleagues they are gay. They are gay in the 'old style.' Sometimes they buy sex in the garden or the park. They buy thirty minutes of pleasure, like you buy pasta or yogurt. Then they are finished being gay. They go back to their lives until the next time. This is how it always was, so they never created a place to live, a ghetto. But now the younger people are slowly coming out, and we don't have that place, that ghetto, and that is good. It's more in the family and not so separate."

Crisafi came out to his Roman mother and his Sicilian father when he was twenty-one. "I had to tell my parents," he says. "My mother hit me. My father said, 'If you are happy like this, it's okay.' Then after a few months they started to change:

My mother was okay with it, and my father was cold toward me. Now my father is sixty-five, my mom is sixty, and they live in Rome. I have a great relationship with them, and they love my boyfriend, Sylvan. My father recently said, 'I'm very happy with you, and I like your boyfriend.' I can't wait to have Christmas, my boyfriend and the nephews all together. For me, it has to be part of the family, because that is what our lives are so much about. The choice is either bringing it into the family, and getting past that crazy moment, or keeping it a big secret—sneaking to the discos or buying your gay life for thirty minutes in the park. And that is just not for me."

Out, **February and March 1998**

THE TRUCK STOPS HERE

TIM AND DALLAS ARE TRUCKERS. They're also cowboys. And they're gay. And this is their piece of the world, High Mountain Ranch and Trucking Company, in remote Newport, Washington, amid the ponderosa pines, bald eagles, moose, and cougars, overlooking the Pend Oreille River on the border of Idaho's panhandle. We're thirty miles from Ruby Ridge, where Randy Weaver had his shoot-out with the FBI, and forty miles from Sandpoint, the headquarters of the evangelical Promise Ministries and the home of Mark Fuhrman of O.J. fame. And somewhere around here is the Aryan Nation compound.

Tim Anderson thirty-two, and his partner of eight years, David "Dallas" Dwight Withrow, thirty-six, chose this area to build this cozy three-bedroom modular cabin. The two men's philosophy has the independent, libertarian spirit of the rural West and the trucker lifestyle. "The gay community sits there in the ghettos and says, 'That's not fair. You don't treat me right,' " Tim opines, his bright green eyes twinkling every time he adds emphasis. "People in the gay community have too much faith that laws are going to make our lives easier. I think laws are complicated and can be abused and manipulated. I don't have faith in it. That does not mean I want to form a gay militia group, but I'm suspicious of the federal government and state government. I don't want those forces involved in my life. I want to make my way through life based on my own merits, and not based on the merits that the state decides on." Toto, we're not in Greenwich Village anymore.

They both grew up in the West, riding horses, and driving trucks. Tim's Native American grandfather was a rodeo star, and his grandmother lived most of her life on a Montana homestead. Dallas was raised on a 2,500-acre Texas ranch and has won a few rodeo titles himself, riding bulls. Their home looks "like a rodeo exploded in it—with a Calvin Klein twist," as one of their friends describes it. Framed photographs and posters of sexy cowboys and mean-looking tractor-trailers line the walls. Over the kitchen cabinets sit miniature covered wagons, several pairs of beat-up cowboy boots, belts, lanterns, cookie tins—even a couple of small bales of hay.

On the one hand, they harbor many traditional values. "I would adopt [a child] in a heartbeat," Dallas says. Dallas's proposal to Tim is the stuff of romance novels: As is the custom among Texans—where a man gets down on his knee and proposes to a woman in front of her parents—Dallas got down on his knee and proposed to Tim in front of Tim's grandparents. They believe gay-rights laws are "too much government," as

Tim says. In this regard, both Tim and Dallas say that as much they don't agree with the philosophies of some of the movements of the West—like Randy Weaver and the militia movements—they do understand the anger and the motives. "Having laws like that just invites the government into your life, just as I feel that antigay laws are too much government too," Tim says. "The government should not have to legislate morality one way or the other."

But just when gay conservatives might claim them, Tim and Dallas put forth views that would delight the gay left. As much as they are committed to each other, they're not so high on same-sex marriage. "I don't think that a piece of paper is going to legitimize our relationship," Tim says. "Every time I have contact with the government, I get screwed up." Dallas is a little more compromising: "I'm torn in the sense that I have in-laws who are antigay, who could come in and take half of my car, my house, my business," he says. "In that sense the legal protection of marriage would be good. But marriage started as a religious institution, and now it's become a way that people have the government validate their relationship, and that I don't agree with." Tim and Dallas defy a lot of perceptions about what being a trucker must be like—let alone what being a *gay* trucker must be like. I will learn a lot more about that over the next couple of days, as I drive truck with them across 1,200 miles of Western highway.

We pack up our things shortly after midnight on a crisp and slightly snowy Saturday night, hop into Tim and Dallas's pickup, and head for Spokane, Washington. At 2:30 A.M. the truckyard in Spokane is desolate. We hop aboard their red Kenworth semitruck, which is leased to a trucking company that arranges their business, getting clients and scheduling pickups and drop-offs. Tim gets into the sleeper part of the cabin, which consists of two bunks, each of which can fit two comfortably. Dallas drives by night, Tim by day.

"This is the brake application gauge," Dallas begins explaining to me, pointing to specific dials on the dashboard. "And this is a four-rear-axle differential temperature gauge, the transmission temperature, air-suspension gauge, the fuel filter restriction gauge, speedometer, tachometer, pyrometer, volt-meter, engine-oil-pressure gauge, turbo-boost gauge, right-hand window, the panel lights . . ." And on and on. When he finishes, he puts the truck in gear, and hollers, "Now let's go for a ride!"

Tim and Dallas met on the road. Tim was hauling potatoes for Frito-Lay, and he spotted Dallas in his truck. The fellow Tim was driving with—someone he was dating—said he thought Dallas was gay. After saying hi to each other at a truck stop, they got on the CB once back on the road and chatted for quite some time, until one of them mentioned the name of a leather bar down in Los Angeles, and the other said he knew of that place.

The rest is history.

It soon becomes clear than unlike the earlier freewheeling times, truckers' schedules are so tight today that they don't have time to hang out much at truck stops with friends. Clients are putting more and more pressure on drivers to cut time. Dispatchers at trucking companies most often even track their truckers via satellite. The company knows their whereabouts at all times, via the satellite, and even knows how fast they're driving. Being monitored like that wouldn't seem to leave room for socializing and meeting people, but they manage.

We stop at a paper mill in Lewiston, Idaho as day just begins to break, an eerie sight as steam rises from all corners of the massive plant. There, we unhook the empty trailer we've hauled from Spokane, and pick up a trailer loaded with paper products, bound for Denver. Once we're out of the valley and up over the mountains, Tim wakes up, preparing to drive. We head back into southern Washington, as we can't take a direct route since big rigs are not allowed on many roads. The CB crackles with something indecipherable.

"Truckers have their own language, their own little nicknames," Tim explains. "It's CB slang, and it changes a lot, particularly when the general public figures it out." Dallas agrees: "Back in the mid-seventies and -eighties, 'good buddy' was a friendship term. Now it's a degrading term, meaning 'fag.' But the gay people will use it amongst themselves. In the truck stops, if they're looking for sex, they'll say over the CB, 'Is there a "good buddy" out there?' " The word for prostitute is "lot lizard," he tells me, and the word for the cruisy rest areas is "pickle parks."

Tim takes over the wheel while Dallas goes to sleep, and we pull into a soft green-and-gold mountain area dominated by wheat farms, near Walla Walla, known as Palouse Country. A few hours later, the vegetation changes dramatically, with sage, juniper, and Douglas firs cropping up. Soon enough, we're driving across the dry and desolate Oregon high desert that stretches into Idaho's flatlands. We pass a rest area known for its cruising, and it sparks conversation. While both Tim and Dallas are far from prudes, and certainly know the cruising sites themselves, they do get annoyed with the industry's reputation among some gays as a haven for people who want hot, anonymous sex. They also don't tolerate people who make sexual remarks when they say they're truckers. They laugh off a publication called *Gay Truckers Classified* that tells people where to find truckers for sex. "That publication is for people who have the fantasy of truckers," Dallas had told me, "but truckers themselves don't read that stuff and don't need to."

Nonetheless, that reputation does draw some people to the industry, looking for an outlaw kind of life—including the sex life—that they've fantasized about with regard to trucking. One former porn actor moved from Baltimore to Tim's ranch to truck.

"When we first went out," he remembers, "we really got along well. But I soon discovered that he didn't want to drive truck because he was in love with the industry. He wanted to drive truck because it made his ego bigger, pulling into a bar with a semitruck, being able to say, 'Hey, I drive truck.' And you can't do that out here. You have a lot of responsibilities. And he was having sex everywhere, in the truck, in the showers [at the truck stops], at the rest stops, constantly. Eventually, he got sick [with AIDS], but he was still partying, and not taking care of himself. He was hanging out in rest area restrooms, or out in the rain, trying to get laid, or going to a smoke-filled bar. His attitude was, 'I don't have any investment in the future, I'm not going to invest in the future,' and that was why he had unprotected sex, too, and didn't seem to care about others."

But tales of the "dark side" of trucking, as Tim calls it, are few and far between. Most of the time Tim and Dallas regale me with stories about gay truckers who befriend them after seeing the rainbow flag sticker on their driver's side window, a lesbian trucker Tim ran with (who pondered transgender surgery) and her beauty-queen girlfriend whom all the men want, creative condom campaigns in the drug stops, CB conversations with closeted rural gay men who sit in their cars on the side of the road, a psychic Native American cowboy woman they worked for who knew they were gay lovers in an instant, and good times at the Habana, a gay hotel and nightclub in Oklahoma City frequented by "truckers, cowboys, drag queens, dance queens, and country people." As we leave the Idaho flatlands,

Tim tells me about someone as colorful—yet perhaps as ominous—as the Utah landscape we're entering. "We were in Alberta and this guy was pulled over in the truck parking area, and I walked up to him and asked him if he needed some help," he begins. "He had these incredibly blue eyes, a gorgeous cowboy.

"Three years later, Dallas ran into him in Oklahoma City. Turns out he was gay and we made friends with him, and we'd talk on the phone and he'd ask us to read from the Damron guide about where all the cruisy places were, 'cause he couldn't have the book on him because he had to go through customs going to Canada. Both Dallas and I would run into him in different places. Then I ran into him in Calgary and we ran together. And that was when he started telling me about this philosophy he has, that the races ought to stay separate and that there shouldn't be intermixing. But he was also vegetarian and despised animal haulers because they were cruel to their horses. His horses were the most important thing to him. He was an animal-rights dude, an Aryan Nation kind of person, and a gay man. He wouldn't socialize in places where black people would. But he'd put his rainbow license plate in the back of his truck, as soon as he got past the border patrol."

We drive through Utah for only a short time, north of Salt Lake City, cutting across northern Utah, heading to Wyoming. As night falls, Dallas takes over the driving, and Tim and I both try to get some shut-eye. But I sleep only a few hours, intermittently hearing a man named Art Bell on the radio, a sort of right-wing psychic, best-selling author and radio talk-show host. Just about the only thing interesting on the radio in the wee hours, Art Bell is someone Tim and Dallas—and many other truckers—listen to often. Bell reads a letter from someone who has just come back from 1999, claiming that another

Clinton scandal will emerge, the "royal oak scandal," and that Clinton will resign not because of the scandals swirling around him but because of health reasons, leaving "President Gore" to run for reelection against Dan Quayle in 2000. We enter Cheyenne, Wyoming, at about 4:00 A.M., and I've come back into the passenger seat, having slept just about all I can, which isn't much. Day breaks again, and we cross the border into Colorado, heading toward Denver, where we'll drop our load. I'm fuzzy, having slept sporadically. I still have Art Bell's premonitions rattling my brain.

It's been a great experience, but as I look out at yet more miles of highway, I find myself clicking my heels and muttering under my breath, "There's no place like home." We pull into a truck stop, and I say my good-byes, getting into a cab, and heading for the depressingly safe and sterile Denver airport, to jet back to New York. Meanwhile, Tim and Dallas gear up and hit the road once again.

Out, **June 1998**

WHAT HAPPENED TO GAY?

IT WAS A YEAR when gay just was not the thing to be. And it was often homosexuals themselves who were running away from the word. Some were said to be too gay, others talked about living post-gay, and still others claimed to be ex-gay. And that was all by mid-July.

The purging of the word "gay" had happened before, most notably back in 1990, when "queer" became all the rage. But this time it was very different. For in 1998, even queer would be considered way too gay, decidedly not post-gay, and the farthest thing from ex-gay. Queer was a hipper, younger, in-your-face way to be gay; it was about being more unique, more homosexual. But too gay, post-gay, and ex-gay, as different as these terms seemed on the surface, all had one striking thing in common: In 1998 people were talking about being *less* homosexual.

By the end of the year, events unfolded that appeared to render these phrases at once meaningless and dangerous, if indeed they hadn't become so already. And we seemed to come back to embracing good old gay, some of us grudgingly, others of us happily. But in the meantime we went on an instructive— if sometimes silly—journey in search of who and what we are.

As with most things these days, it all began on TV. At the top of 1998, the ABC sitcom *Ellen,* starring Ellen DeGeneres, was struggling to stay on the air, the heady days of magazine covers and White House parties having long since evaporated. After a few highly rated hilarious episodes at the end of 1997, Ellen's ratings began taking a dive. DeGeneres and *Ellen's* lead character, Ellen Morgan, were both still in the throes of coming out, and the show was rife with inside jokes only homosexuals could truly understand. As ABC was floating rumors of the show's imminent demise, DeGeneres was spinning out episode after episode that seemed to have the same theme: I am lesbian, hear me roar. DeGeneres, along with her newfound love, actress Anne Heche, had become an activist, and we were blessed to have such a high-profile person speaking up for our rights. But, notwithstanding Kate Clinton and a couple of other people, there's one problem with activists, particularly those who are overcome by the passions of the new convert: They're often not very funny. And as Ellen DeGeneres became more like Joan of Arc meets Stonewall, the laugh quotient went down.

Enter Chastity Bono. As a spokesperson for the Gay and Lesbian Alliance Against Defamation (GLAAD), she gave an interview to a *Daily Variety* reporter just as the rumors of ABC's desire to kill the show had reached a crescendo. The article quoted Bono as saying the problem with *Ellen* was that it had become "too gay," though Bono has steadfastly denied that she used those exact words in trying to make her larger point: that the show's content was too focused on Ellen's lesbian experience for straight Americans to be able to relate well to it.

The day after the article ran, March 10, TOO GAY blared from headlines in newspapers from coast to coast and became the hot topic on radio talk shows and on tabloid TV.

Poor Ellen. Many believe that Bono's alleged remarks were the final nail in the coffin for the sitcom, which was canceled at the end of the season. Poor Chastity, too. If DeGeneres had lost her show, Bono soon lost her job, resigning from GLAAD despite her and the group's insistence that her remarks had been misrepresented. Bono also lost a lot of credibility among many gay men and lesbians and became the object of ridicule, bitterly attacked by such heavy hitters as Lea DeLaria.

There's no question that, from a tactical point of view, as the spokesperson for a group that had a vested interest in keeping *Ellen* on the air, Bono had made a blunder by trying to offer a complex analysis within the context of the sound-bite world of the media. A lot of straight people, including straight journalists, are so uncomfortable with homosexuality that they often do in fact think homosexuals are too gay. It would be easy and tempting for a reporter to put words in her mouth and float out "too gay" if offered even a little bit of room to do so. And such a quote could only affect the show's future in a detrimental way.

Though she might have been trying to make a valid point about the show's appeal to straights, as she later told the *Advocate,* Bono also may have been gesturing toward something that most gay people have come to know well. And perhaps that was why, though she angered a lot of gay men and lesbians, many other gay people wholeheartedly agreed with her "too gay" critique—

whether she said it so plainly or not. After all, we all privately have our own ideas about what too gay is. For some of us, it's people who talk incessantly about their homosexuality, as if it were their raison d'être ("My being gay is such an innate part of my inner core—did I tell you I was gay?"). For others, too gay is reserved for those who are patriotic toward the cause in a way that seems crass and tacky: the people who wear cheesy rainbow everything and sport T-shirts like "I'm not gay but my boyfriend is." For still others, "too gay" is the term used to describe those who plunge into the "gay lifestyle," which we all know really does exist: lesbians who move to Northampton, grow lots of hair on their bodies, and measure the size of their vibrators, and gay men who move to West Hollywood, wax all the hair off their bodies, and measure the size of their . . . muscles.

In 1998 the gay party circuit was dubbed too gay. Pride was too gay. The Dinah Shore golf tournament was too gay (well, too lesbian). Restaurants with postmodern decor and pounding house music were too gay. Barbra Streisand and Bette Midler, as always, were way too gay—even though they're straight. And yes, in that vein, *Ellen* was too gay.

If Andy Warhol were alive, he might say that every gay or lesbian person will be too gay for fifteen minutes. We all grow up in the closet, living a lie. When we come out, we often break down our closets like gangbusters. Before we settle in comfortably, we spend a lot of time focusing on our homosexuality. We often challenge everyone and everything, weaving our sexuality into every single aspect of our lives, even if it sometimes seems a bit forced. That's exactly what Ellen DeGeneres and Ellen Morgan were doing.

Judging from the show, for DeGeneres, the experience was quite cathartic. But to a lot of straight people, it was too insider to be entertaining. And while it was something exhilarating for those lesbians and gay men who might have been just stepping out of the closet as well (or were still closeted), to a lot of gay people who'd been out for many years, it was just dull: They'd been there, done that.

Without a doubt, there's a certain smugness in the too-gay critique. It reminds me of how my family would subtly look down on their relatives back in southern Italy: They were still too Italian, while we had arrived. Too gay underscores the fact that almost thirty years into the post-Stonewall gay-rights movement, we are all at very different stages in our coming-out, with varying degrees of allegiance to the gay-ghetto value system and political viewpoint. That was always true, perhaps, but in 1998 we were focusing more on these differences among us than on our commonalities. Fierce arguments broke out among activists over how we present ourselves to the public and how we define ourselves to one another.

A virtual civil war erupted, for example, when the gay-founded Universal Fellowship of Metropolitan Community Churches and the Washington, D.C.–based Human Rights Campaign, the largest gay-rights advocacy group, early in the year announced plans for a Millennium March on Washington. Other grassroots activists accused the groups of trying to exclude input from a broad coalition and trying to direct the march in such a way that would be more acceptable to straights, such as by not having the words "gay," "lesbian," "bisexual," and "transgendered" in the name of the march—in other words, not appearing too gay. Later in the year HRC came under intense criticism again when, in the U.S. Senate race in New York, it endorsed the Republican incumbent, Alfonse D'Amato, who was a staunch opponent of abortion and affirmative action but had supported gay rights in a few instances. His Democratic challenger, Rep. Charles Schumer, won the election with the overwhelming support of the gay community, garnering 77 percent of the gay vote to D'Amato's 14 percent (according to Voter News Service). Even New York's Governor George Pataki, a pro-choice Republican who was reelected, garnered 31 percent of the gay vote. HRC's message to Congress was simple: We are no longer too gay to support an antichoice Republican, breaking from our historical connection to the women's movement. But in voting the way they did, perhaps the message from New York's lesbians and gay men to HRC— and to Congress as well—as even simpler: Yes, we are.

In 1998 these and many other disagreements played out in the mainstream media, in the gay press, and, perhaps most vociferously, on the Internet, and all similarly seemed to focus on how gay we were going to stay, how committed we would remain to the values that had been set and defined over the years within the gay movement. Everyone seemed to agree that some of these values needed to change. But we disagreed on which ones to keep and which ones to throw out.

One reason we had the luxury this year to engage in spirited —if sometimes divisive—debates to discuss things as seemingly silly as whether we were too gay was because we had lost a common focus: Death and disease, quite thankfully, were no longer drawing many of us together.

In August, San Francisco's *Bay Area Reporter,* a local weekly newspaper, for the first time in seventeen years did not have any obituaries to print, a fact that was celebrated and written about across the country. Throughout the year the media were filled with stories showing the dramatic drop in deaths due to AIDS, all thanks to the new combinations of drugs that have now been in widespread use among gay men with HIV for the past two years.

Some of us were trying to temper this often-simplified

sound-bite news, fearing that it might dangerously fuel complacency toward the epidemic, which was—and is—far from over. Still, for many people, particularly younger people who had not experieced the horrors of the late-1980s AIDS epidemic, absence of death was enough to have them believe that "the AIDS crisis is over," as gay sex-advice columnist Dan Savage told the *Village Voice* in October. It appeared that AIDS itself, having been around for eighteen years, was also now too gay. For many, it was time to move beyond it—whether the epidemic was over or not.

An eerie apathy, coupled with an ignorance of recent history, seemed to set in by 1998. And the apathy wasn't just around AIDS. Gay-rights activism in general seemed to be in a dormant stage, with many people appearing to believe we'd arrived. It was true there was more cultural acceptance than ever before, on television, in films, and in the media, and we had reason to be proud. But politically, we had a long and arduous road ahead. In stunningly positive news, the state of Georgia surprised us all this year when it overturned its sodomy statute, but nineteen states still have sodomy laws on the books; only eleven states outlaw discrimination against gays (and a federal antidiscrimination bill is a long way off); gay-inclusive hate-crimes bills languished in state legislatures and in Congress; and we lost referenda on gay marriage in Alaska and Hawaii. And Trent Lott, the majority leader of the U.S. Senate, clearly had his own definition of too gay, likening us to kleptomaniacs.

Indeed, in much of 1998 the gay movement appeared to be overcome by the glass half empty/glass half full syndrome. Perhaps the booming economy didn't help in this regard. Many lesbian and gay Americans, like all Americans, were living it up, and escapism was the order of the day. For them, it was not a time to worry about politics, and it was most certainly party time once again. Many gay men plunged into the sex-and-drugs scene, causing the international gay party circuit to grow even more dramatically in 1998. But while apathy had many individuals submerging themselves farther into the ghetto, it had some gay people going the other way, seeing it all as, yes, just a bit too gay. They walled themselves off, in the cities and beyond, seeing no reason to relate to a gay community any longer, eschewing the commercialism and conformity that had taken hold, shrugging off gay identity.

Post-gay slithered onto the scene, attempting to capitalize on this prevalent apathy and have its own fifteen minutes—even if it got only roughly thirty seconds. It was in March that Londoner James Collard, former editor of the British gay magazine *Attitude,* took the reins as editor of *Out* magazine, bringing his post-gay philosophy with him. On its arrival on these shores, however, post-gay was a murky concept and one that never really became clear. As I understood it, in Britain "post-gay" was another name for what was sarcastically and ironically known as the antigay movement there, a movement in which gay people rejected the consumeristic and commercial trappings of the gay ghetto. Though it was rather amorphous, there were some interesting intellectual points that antigay and post-gay raised about conformity in thought, values, look, and lifestyle. Unfortunately, the open-endedness and ambiguity of the terms also allowed for people to use them to their own advantage, to claim intellectual underpinning for what was nothing but political complacency, or to use them in a variety of other ways.

In the case of *Out* magazine, it seemed that the plan was to use post-gay as a marketing tool. Any intellectual gimmick, however, needs a compelling leader, and from the start Collard just didn't seem to have it in him. At a symposium at New York City's New School University in May, Collard explained that post-gay "began in the better London nightclubs" and was about "getting beyond the ghetto." Last time anyone checked, however, the better nightclubs were very much a part of the ghetto. Rather than fully explaining himself, Collard often strangely left it to others to figure out what post-gay is, based on statements he'd made. He had, for example, expressed outright disgust for certain gay bars and symbols, and he seemed to harbor a disdain for activism.

By all accounts, *Out*'s previous editor, Sarah Pettit, was fired, in part, because she was, well, too gay. The magazine's backers apparently believed *Out* had become too serious and issue-driven and needed to focus more on fun, young, hip content so as to boost circulation. It appeared that they were looking to post-gay as a way to exploit the new apolitical mood that had people rejecting gay identity and turning away from politics. And this less strident, less serious tack could only be more popular with straight (and gay) advertisers as well.

But while post-gay appeared as if it just might be able to cash in on the apathy, in a relatively short time it was floundering. Months after the term was introduced, one was hard-pressed to find many Americans who would call themselves "post-gay." People who may have been rejecting the word "gay" because, among other things, it had become too much of a created, commercialized identity label, were not about to latch on to yet another label, particularly one that was being marketed to them in a similarly aggressive way.

But the greatest problem for post-gay was simply that other forces began to converge on the horizon that would further muddy its already-muddy message. The ex-gay movement burst onto the scene, thoroughly confusing a lot of people about the terms. Collard took another stab at explaining post-gay in an issue of *Newsweek* devoted to coverage of ex-gays. And that is perhaps what caused more than one television commentator to use the term "post-gay" when describing the ex-gay movement.

The ex-gay movement and the way it was catapulted to the center of media attention after having been on the fringes was like a bad dream. But in a strange way, even if it was a mere coincidence, it seemed like ex-gay's sudden emergence was a natural, if ironic, progression of our focus on too gay and the drive to be post-gay—a chilling-but-funny slap in the face. If you're going through all kinds of machinations to distance yourself from gay, after all, why not take that extra step and simply go straight?

For many of us, the ex-gay movement seemed so out-to-lunch that it was hard to take seriously. It was in July that ads began appearing in major newspapers telling people that they could change their sexuality, that they could become heterosexual and drop out of the gay "lifestyle." Most prominent among the ex-gays of 1998 were Anne and John Paulk, a smiling married couple. She claimed to be a former lesbian (though it would later be revealed that she was perhaps never a lesbian), and he claimed to be a former gay man who was also a drag queen—and he had the photos to prove it. It was, to say the least, bizarre to imagine John Paulk as a porky drag queen strutting in a Midwest nightclub and now view him as the picture of heterosexual bliss. It was this kind of incredibility, coupled with most out gay people's awareness that it's ridiculous to think people can actually change, that made many of us believe, naïvely, that the ads were benign.

To be sure, on the one hand the ads were a definitive measure of our success. The religious-right groups that sponsored and promoted the ads had realized they needed a new strategy—a kinder, gentler face. The ads were about having "compassion" for the poor homosexuals rather than attacking them as bringing all kinds of evil upon the planet. These nice religious folks were now going to save us rather than banish us. That the religious right realized that outright hate and bile didn't work as well any longer showed how successful the gay movement had become by 1998. We have been able to defuse attacks simply by being visible and vocal and showing that we're not the three-headed child molesters our enemies claimed we were.

However, even the right's new "caring" strategy seemed not to fly in the court of public opinion. The media were quick to focus on the ex-gay ads, which became front-page news. Almost all summer newspaper articles and radio and television talk shows discussed the dubiousness of being able to convert one's sexuality from homo to hetero. The pundits weighed in, and we were almost universally supported, as the religious right found itself increasingly isolated. Polls, too, were showing that a majority of Americans believed that one could not change from homosexual to heterosexual.

On the other hand the ads were very dangerous in a way that many of us who'd been out for a long time were not quick to grasp. Maybe that was further indication of the apathy that had set in, but it was quite obvious that the ads had some potentially harmful effects. Within the context of a grossly homophobic culture, the ads could seduce conflicted, closeted people, young and old, into believing they could and should change, doing them a lot of psychological damage. More detrimental, by condemning homosexuality to the point of actually offering to help people to convert from it, the ads could further empower those who hate gays and could enable some to go to any lengths to stop us. The reality of what hatred—even kinder, gentler hatred—emitted into the public consciousness could do hadn't dawned on many until early October, when the gruesome murder in Laramie, Wyoming, of twenty-one-year-old Matthew Shepard stunned the world.

What else can be said about the murder and the vigils and protest marches in response to it that occurred across America? At this point, almost everything is a cliché. It shocked us. It frightened us. It galvanized us. It invigorated us. All that is true. But Matthew Shepard's murder also reminded us of who and what we are—to ourselves and to much of the rest of the world. It underscored the very real presence of physical violence in each of our lives. Shepard's was not the first nor the most horrific gay-bashing this year. Nor was small-town America the only place such violence was occurring. New York City gay activists had been pointing to a surge in gay-bashing all year, long before the Shepard murder, and San Francisco, Los Angeles, and other cities regularly see antigay violence. But maybe because Matthew Shepard was a middle-class college student who was cute and white and from the heartland, the media were quick to focus on his story. The power of television can't be underestimated: The image of the fence where Shepard was tied and left to die was beamed over and over into our homes and dragged many gay men and lesbians into the harsh reality of our lives on city streets and well beyond every day.

Suddenly the too-gay critique seemed like a self-indulgent and silly game. Ex-gay was seen for all of the danger that it truly represents. And the subsequent activism and awareness the murder sparked appeared to be the death knell for post-gay. Matthew Shepard's murder reminded us that we never freely took on these labels for ourselves, and thus we can't just freely reject them, as if we don't live within a homophobic society. Whether homosexual, gay, queer, fag, dyke, lezzie, he-she, or what have you, these terms were either chosen for us a long, long time ago by our enemies, or we decided upon them because we were forced to respond to our enemies' marking us as different and deviant. We may one day be post-gay, when America ceases to separate us out and label us in ways that bring discrimination and violence upon our lives. But in 1998 we learned that, in the meantime and probably for a very long time, we are still gay.

The Advocate, **January 19, 1999**

OUTING BY ANY OTHER NAME

IN 1990 THE WORD "outing" suddenly took on a new, fearful connotation. In the mainstream media's definition—the only definition to which most people were exposed—outing meant revealing that a public figure was gay or lesbian against his or her will, something that many a columnist described as akin to McCarthyism.

At the time, I was among the people being tarred as a proponent of outing because I advocated that the media honestly report on gay public figures' lives in the same way they report on straight public figures' lives. As far as I was concerned, this was "reporting"—or, as some of my colleagues described it, "equalizing." But the word "outing" and its negative connotation couldn't be shaken off.

Today, not much has changed in that regard: Outing is still thought by many in the media to be something aggressive and wrong, and many reputable media organizations claim to have a policy against it. The one unmistakable difference now, however, is that those same media organizations actually regularly engage in one form of outing or another, although they're loath to admit it. In fact, in the year 2000, apart from the supermarket tabloids, the leading practitioners of what was dubbed "outing" in 1990 are not activists and gay-media journalists but those same mainstream media powers that once lined up to condemn the practice. And that, paradoxically, is both a measure of the power of words and of the enormous progress that American culture and journalism have made on the issue of disclosing one's homosexuality.

It was *Time* magazine that coined the term "outing" back in 1990, creating an active, even somewhat violent, verb to describe my commentary. In my "Gossip Watch" column at the now-defunct *OutWeek*—a weekly gay and lesbian magazine with an activist bent—I was pointing out how much of the media glamorized heterosexuality and hid homosexuality: They made sure to accurately report every intimate detail about heterosexual celebrities' and politicians' lives—whether the subjects wanted such facts reported or not—but they willingly lied about public figures who were gay, printing stories about alleged dalliances with members of the opposite sex when they often knew such tales were figments of publicists' imaginations. I often corrected the mainstream media's inaccuracies in my column, of course printing the names of the people to whom I was referring.

The AIDS epidemic was mushrooming in those years, and the urgency of gay visibility was being underscored by activists while the silence around AIDS in the media and among politicians was deafening. The closeted gay Hollywood heartthrob Rock Hudson had died of AIDS-related causes a few years earlier, and his life and death exposed how the media bought into the Hollywood machine that heterosexualized actors—and how that machine reflected an entrenched media hypocrisy that went well beyond Hollywood.

What was the rationale among mainstream journalists to promote such inaccuracies, I asked. They were protecting people's right to privacy, they claimed, noting that it was up to the individual to decide whether or not to be out or to put forth a heterosexual facade and that no one else could make that decision. And at that time, make no mistake, suggesting or even hinting that someone was gay was considered as horrific as outright reporting it. (One particular list of well-known names printed in an early edition of *OutWeek* was quickly mythologized into a scandalous catalog of the celebrity closet even though the names were published without any accompanying comment about the celebrities' sexuality.) Indeed, simply asking an individual point-blank about his or her sexual orientation was considered a cruel and terroristic form of interviewing. It was all outing, pure and simple.

I smelled homophobia. After all, there the mainstream media were, reporting all the intimate details of the multimillionaire developer Donald Trump's divorce and extramarital affairs and throwing questions at him left and right while simultaneously lecturing us piously about "privacy." I charged that the real reason they were attacking me and others who supported similar reporting on gay public figures was because they thought even being a homosexual, and revealing that fact, was the most horrible thing in the world.

Rather than engaging in healthy debate and presenting my opinions in a responsible manner, however, most of the mainstream media elected to demonize me and others as neo–Fascists hell-bent on destruction.

In fact, when I wrote a lengthy article about New York's other multimillionaire of the day—publishing tycoon Malcolm Forbes—shortly after he died in February 1990, all hell broke loose. At first the media tried to suppress the story, but their own desire to sell papers got the best of them. So they reported on it—sometimes using Forbes's name, sometimes still closeting him as an unnamed, recently deceased publishing tycoon, as if people couldn't guess who that was—while simultaneously attacking me for writing the story, often charging that I was the gay community's new worst enemy. The media's sudden concern for the welfare of homosexuals—at a time when the media rarely focused on gay and lesbian issues and often did so only with a homophobic spin—was as suspect as their concerns about privacy.

In truth, mainstream journalists hated outing because it was a critique of them: It was telling them that they were doing their jobs wrong, treating gay public figures and straight public figures unequally. And it was calling them on their homophobia. For me, it was a painful time, but it was also exhilarating because I knew we were kicking off a debate that would go on for years, finally letting a genie out of the bottle.

Ten years later, that genie is hard at work—and now in the mainstream media. In recent years, the *Wall Street Journal* broke news of Jann Wenner's same-sex love affair, and *Esquire* magazine plopped Kevin Spacey on its cover with the caption KEVIN SPACEY HAS A SECRET and a story that begins, " 'Kevin Spacey?' my mom said. . . . 'Well, I hear he's gay.' " And just in December, Andrew Sullivan, often described in the early

1990s as a gay conservative, named names in his *New York Times Magazine* column.

This was the same Sullivan who, in a 1990 article titled "Sleeping with the Enemy" in *The New Republic,* wrote that outers "have attacked the central protection of gay people themselves," observing that the "gleam in the eye of the outers" is "the gleam of the authoritarian."

By the time of his *New York Times Magazine* column in 1999 Sullivan had done a 180-degree turn. In chastising such individuals as Rosie O'Donnell, Ricky Martin, Secretary of Health and Human Services Donna Shalala, Attorney General Janet Reno, Gore campaign manager Donna Brazile, former New York City mayor Ed Koch, and fitness guru Richard Simmons because they refuse to declare their sexual orientation, Sullivan opined:

> There comes a point, surely, at which the diminishing public stigmatization of homosexuality makes this kind of coyness not so much understandably defensive as simply feeble: insulting to homosexuals, who know better, and condescending to heterosexuals, who deserve better. It's as if the closet has had every foundation and bearing wall removed but still stands, supported by mere expediency, etiquette and the lingering shards of shame. Does no one have the gumption just to blow it down?

And when Koch fumed to the *New York Post* the following week that Sullivan is like "the Jew-catcher of Nazi Germany," it certainly brought back memories for me; the difference this time around, however, was that few other prominent voices came to Koch's defense.

The liberal friend of gays Barbara Walters, meanwhile,

wouldn't relent when interviewing Ricky Martin on her ABC-TV Oscar-night special in March. After Martin evaded her first inquiry about "rumors that question and talk about [his] sexual orientation," Walters pushed on: "You could say, as many artists have, 'Yes, I am gay,' or you could say, 'No, I'm not.' " And when Martin continued to dodge the question, Walters—sounding every bit like an activist—said, "It's in your power to do it." Martin was forced to feebly utter, "I understand . . . [but] I just don't feel like it."

There's more. In her March 2000 book, *Dish: The Inside Story on the World of Gossip,* MSNBC.com columnist Jeannette Walls discusses the sexual orientation of the cybergossip Matt Drudge. Seeing it as relevant to the story of Drudge's own reporting on private lives, Walls interviewed several men who say they dated him, and spoke to former friends who knew him as gay, such as Dan Mathews, campaign director of People for the Ethical Treatment of Animals.

Each of the above instances—speculating, asking, and outright reporting—would have been dubbed "outing" ten years ago, attacked by pundits of media outlets such as the *New York Times* and ABC-TV as the worst breach of privacy. Today, however, these practices have simply been folded into journalism. What we did in the gay press has clearly pointed the way for many at today's mainstream outlets. "Equalizing" has, in many cases, become reality. Yet the word "outing" itself continues to be demonized, with only the supermarket tabloids now proudly acknowledging that they out people (something even they didn't trumpet prior to 1990). Fearful of being tarred, the mainstream journalists I've mentioned would no doubt insist—as Andrew Sullivan defensively, and somewhat laughably, even stated in his aforementioned *New York Times Magazine* article—"I don't believe in outing people."

Much like the word "feminist" or the word "liberal," the word "outing" became so politicized and reviled that it couldn't possibly be accepted—even as the broad practice it was invented to describe continues, slowly but surely, to become a part of mainstream journalism. Ask women on the street if they are feminists, and they'll likely say no more often than not. But ask them if they support equal pay for women, abortion rights, and sexual autonomy, and they'll likely say yes a lot more often. That change in attitudes is the real measure of the feminist movement—not the acceptance of the word "feminist" itself.

The same is true of outing: Most gay people may say they're opposed to outing, but ask them if it's right for a public figure's homosexuality to be reported on—or at least questioned—when it is relevant to a larger story, and most will probably agree. And that attitude is the real measure of how far equal reporting on gay public figures has come in the past ten years.

The Advocate, **August 15, 2000**

CYBER MECCA

THE GREATEST EXAMPLE THUS far of the Internet's power has to be its ability to swiftly draw together on a global scale members of one of the most underground subcultures imaginable: lesbian and gay Muslims.

Just five years ago, the thought of gay Muslims organizing at the international level was unfathomable. In many devoutly Muslim countries, after all, homosexuality is a crime punishable by death. In Iran, Iraq, and Afghanistan, men who've engaged in homosexual acts have often been cruelly tortured and executed—in the name of Islam. In other Muslim countries, people are imprisoned for life for being gay; known lesbians are often shunned by society forever. It's not difficult to understand why many lesbians and gay men in the Muslim world would remain deeply in hiding—nor how the Internet has now become a sort of miraculous lifeline.

"I don't see any other way that queer Muslims could be reached," says Sulayman X, who runs a Web site called Queer Jihad. "You certainly couldn't put an ad in the *Baghdad Times*." Queer Jihad offers provocative, engaging essays and articles by writers worldwide as well as readers' comments. The site also provides numerous links to gay, Islamic, Arabic, and Asian cultural, legal, and political sites.

Sulayman X, who converted to Islam in 1993, is a journalist who lives in a large Asian city; he does not use his given name for fear of retribution. Ever since he created Queer Jihad in 1997, the response has been staggering—from gay and lesbian Muslims as well as from those who hate them. "The most overwhelming response has been sheer disgust," he recounts sadly. "I get e-mail every day from Muslims who are offended, disgusted, outraged, can't believe there's any such thing as a gay Muslim, and all the rest of it."

Like gay and lesbian Christians in this country who are embroiled in their own war with the religious right, Sulayman X and other gay Muslims maintain that Islam is being misused. "Islam is an elegant, simple religion that values humankind and places much emphasis on the here and now—creating just societies," he says. "Islam has been hijacked by extremists, and when you read about Muslims in the newspaper, invariably it's about Muslims who are killing people or resorting to violence to get what they want. But that's not Islam. That's people using Islam as a political tool to achieve political ends."

The barrage of hate e-mail Sulayman X receives every day, he says, is offset by reactions he gets from gay and lesbian Muslims who stumble onto the site. "What makes it all worthwhile are the occasional good responses: when a gay or lesbian

Muslim writes and says, 'Hey, I thought I was the only one!' There've also been several from young people wanting to commit suicide and others from young men trapped in marriages they didn't want."

To Sulayman X, who has recently written articles for publication in U.S. gay newspapers by sending them out via the Internet, the new technology is providing a way to bridge cultures and bring the gay Muslim experience to the surface. "Almost overnight, we now have a safe way to connect," he explains, "to explore this issue, to talk about our lives."

One site that Queer Jihad links to is that of the New York–based Al-Fatiha Foundation, which was itself created on the Internet. The organization grew out of an e-mail discussion group—or Listserv—for "gay, lesbian, bisexual, transgendered, and questioning" Muslims, founded in 1997 by Faisal Alam, a twenty-two-year-old Washington, D.C., activist.

"It was the first time that communication was made possible by gay Muslims across the world," Faisal notes. The Listserv soon grew to include subscribers from twenty-five countries. By 1998 small gatherings of subscribers began taking place, and Al-Fatiha was thus formed. Soon enough, in 1998 the group held an international conference in Boston. And in May the organization will hold in London the Second International Retreat for LGBTQ Muslims and Their Friends.

People from as far away as Singapore and Pakistan have expressed interest in attending. "We are in communication with gay and lesbian groups in countries like Turkey and Malaysia, where one would not imagine that such groups are organizing," Alam says. "They all want Al-Fatiha chapters to open up in their areas, and with the help of the Internet, that dream will come true."

The Advocate, **March 14, 2000**

A WORLDWIDE FIRST:
A TRANSSEXUAL PARLIAMENT

IF THE SPIRIT OF Stonewall—where drag queens were said to have led riots in the streets of New York City—seems to have swept rapidly across America over the past thirty years, it has often raced at an even quicker pace in other countries, where political and cultural realities allow for quite different outcomes.

Take, for example, the tiny country of New Zealand, where forty-two-year-old Georgina Beyer, mayor of the town of Carterton for the past four years, in November became the first transgendered member of Parliament—of any parliament in the world.

"Stonewall had a big effect on New Zealand and on gay liberation," Beyer says from her new offices in Wellington, New

Zealand's capital. The irony, she points out, is that the United States, which gave birth to Stonewall, has now fallen behind many other countries in guaranteeing civil rights for sexual minorities. "I find that in America, as one of the most free countries in the world with respect to the whole broad arena of gay, lesbian, bisexual, and transgender rights, people still have to fight hard for things that we seem to have gotten quite easily. Maybe it is because America is so huge that it is harder."

New Zealand, with a population of just under 4 million, passed national human-rights legislation banning discrimination against lesbians, gays, and people with HIV in housing and employment in 1993, only seven years after sex between consenting male adults was decriminalized. It is one of only a handful of countries that allows foreign partners of its gay and lesbian citizens to immigrate to its shores and become naturalized citizens. And New Zealand's new prime minister, Helen Clark, is now talking about legalizing same-sex marriage. And while there are antigay religious zealots in New Zealand just as everywhere else, such hatemongers have little political power.

Beyer's journey has been symbolic of New Zealand's own progress. Part Maori, New Zealand's native people, she grew up as George Beyer on a farm in the bucolic Taranaki region. As a young man she acted on a TV soap opera in Wellington. But when she began going out in drag to Wellington's gay nightclubs, the producers told her she needed to tone it down. That was not something she was willing to do. She left the show, fell on hard times, and even turned briefly to prostitution.

During that period of her life, while in Sydney, Australia, she was brutally raped by four men one night. Understandably, it was a life-changing experience. "It damaged me emotionally, and it gave me reason to reassess my life," she says. "I ended up developing fire in my belly."

She moved back to more film and television dered roles—and starte gender-reassignment surg to the tiny rural town involved in politics, earni community. She lost her 1992 by only 14 votes, the later. She was elected mayo to run for member of Parl

Perhaps the most interes tory is that the mere fact o member of Parliament does "New Zealanders are tolerar cated on these issues, the mo Beyer notes, though she's ca don't want for a minute to who find [homosexuality an cautions. "But things have be

"I believe it will take anot ative behavior against gays to humbly when asked what a activists. "Part of the way to o out the error of the ways of our gay communities must ab and dignity."

T

BENEVOLENT HATEMONGERS

STANDING ON HIS BALCONY overlooking St. Peter's Square this summer, Pope John Paul II unleashed a tirade against gays and lesbians that received international press coverage. The pope was furious because World Pride Rome 2000, a week of gay-pride events that included a march, occurred in his own backyard despite his having used all the powers of the Vatican for months to try to shut it down. The Italian government withdrew its support as a result, yet World Pride was ultimately successful, garnering enormous positive attention—thanks in no small part to the publicity surrounding John Paul II's crusade against it.

"In the name of the Church of Rome, I must express sadness for the affront to the Grand Jubilee of the year 2000 and for the offense to the Christian values of a city that is so dear to the hearts of the Catholics of the world," the pope said on the day after the World Pride march, addressing tens of thousands of pilgrims after celebrating a mass for prisoners. "Homosexual acts are against nature's laws. The church cannot silence the truth, because this would not help discern what is good from what is evil." He then called homosexuality "objectively disordered."

It was nothing but pure, unadulterated hate speech—grade-A homophobia and bigotry couched in religious theology in the manner of Pat Robertson and Jerry Falwell. John Paul II has long shown his intolerance by his repeated threatening and silencing of clergy who reach out to gay Catholics, but by uttering these words so vehemently and so publicly, he revealed before the whole world that he is a hateful man with little regard for the discrimination and violence he brings upon people's lives.

Like all hatred, the pope's is anchored in fear. Perhaps it has something to do with what the historian Garry Wills, in his current best-seller *Papal Sin,* describes as John Paul's "panic at the perception that the priesthood is becoming predominantly gay."

But it is hatred nonetheless—no different from Stalin's or even Hitler's. It's the same hate that motivates Jesse Helms, David Duke, and even the Atlanta Braves' John Rocker. But the fact that the pope is a virulent hatemonger is something that religious and political leaders don't dare admit—though they may agree privately—lest they be labeled attackers of the all-powerful Catholic Church.

And committed Catholics, gay or straight, find it difficult to accept that the pope inspires hate. He is, they point out, the leader of a church with a mission to love and nurture everyone. "As a Catholic, it's hard to find the pope is a hateful man," says

Marianne Duddy, executive director of Dignity/USA, an organization for gay Catholics, who are shunned by the church. "There's so much that he does that's good. Thinking of him that way is difficult. You want to believe that it's motivated by something less vicious than hate."

But it doesn't matter what good Pope John Paul does in the world; many a dictator of the past had a beneficent heart for select people while simultaneously condemning entire groups, passively or actively facilitating murder against them. Scapegoating minority groups is in fact one way that such autocratic leaders maintain control over the masses.

Sometimes, it seems, it takes another hatemonger to point to the elephant in the room: "I don't see StopthePope.com," embattled talk-show host Laura Schlessinger, a.k.a. "Dr. Laura," told the *New York Times* in discussing the pontiff's remarks, alluding to the anti-Schlessinger Web site StopDrLaura.com. (Of course, gay activists, ever industrious, soon rectified that situation: StopthePope.com now links to sites that deal with homosexuality and religion.)

For once, Schlessinger made a sterling point. There's little difference between her calling homosexuality a "biological error" and the pope's calling it "objectively disordered." Both statements demonize gay people as abnormal, perhaps even dangerous. At best, these statements equally bolster homophobes in their desire to continue discriminating against gays. At worst, they embolden gay-bashers to continue their violence on the streets.

Yet while the pope's words are more widely publicized and carry far more weight than Schlessinger's—he is spiritual leader for tens of millions, after all—no companies have distanced themselves from the Catholic Church, as companies like Procter & Gamble and Sears have done with Schlessinger. Few politicians have spoken up, and those who did—such as openly gay Washington, D.C., city councilmember Jim Graham—were accused of "Catholic bashing." The Reverend Penny Nixon, openly lesbian copastor of San Francisco's Metropolitan Community Church, called the pope's words "an incredible misuse of power" that will result in "beaten, bruised, and battered bodies," but she was a lone voice among religious leaders. Where were the voices of Catholic leaders, from bishops to priests to nuns, who disagree with the pope? Where were the supportive and liberal Jewish and Protestant religious leaders who have been quick to speak up against Schlessinger's hate, which is also expressed in the name of faith (in her case, Orthodox Judaism)?

Where, indeed, was Dignity/USA? The group released a statement that described the pope's words as "extremely offensive and unnecessarily antagonistic," but failed to discuss the consequences of such defamation. Indeed, Duddy continues to split hairs in order to separate the pope from other homophobes, such as Schlessinger. "Someone who is using the public airwaves for commercial success has a different set of motivations than a religious leader," she says. "I think there's a distinction in the language that is used. The pope's rhetoric is not as vitriolic as Jerry Falwell's and Pat Robertson's has been in the past."

"This was Dignity's golden opportunity, and they blew it," says veteran New York journalist and *LGNY* columnist Andy Humm, one of the few critics in the media, straight or gay, to speak out. "This was an opportunity to pull in other Christians, nuns, priests to stand up and say, 'You can't do this'—to put Catholic politicians on the spot, from Ted Kennedy and Mario Cuomo to Rudy Giuliani and Rick Lazio. Where are the Catholic-led public protests over these vile slurs from their leader?"

Until there are public protests—as well as widespread, sustained, and loud condemnation from Catholics and non-Catholics alike—the pope and his successors will continue to silence good people through fear and intimidation while simultaneously endangering all of our lives.

The Advocate, **September 12, 2000**

Note: Pope John Paul II died in April 2005. Anyone hoping for reform in the Catholic Church after his death, however, was grandly disappointed when the German prelate Cardinal Josef Ratzinger was selected as his successor, Pope Benedict XVI. As the head of the Congregation of the Doctrine of the Faith, Ratzinger was the Vatican's homophobic brain trust, writing all of John Paul's most stinging antigay pronouncements, including the statement that homosexuality is "intrinsically evil."

HATE CRIMES: LIKE THE TALIBAN, AMERICA'S MIDDLE EAST ALLIES TYRANNIZE GAYS AND WOMEN

ON MARCH 22, 1998, eighteen-year-old Abdul Sami and another young man, a twenty-two-year-old named Bismillah, were buried alive—put beside a mud wall that was bulldozed upon them—inside a stadium in the Afghan city of Herat.

The gruesome public execution was the young men's sentence, under Taliban law, of having been found guilty of engaging in sodomy. They were hardly the first to receive that kind of punishment for same-sex sexual transgressions: Just one month earlier, three men found guilty of the same infraction had a stone wall collapsed on them in public just outside the city of Kandahar (purported to have had a large homosexual community before the Taliban seized power in 1996). Amazingly, all three survived and were taken to the hospital with fractures of most of the bones in their bodies; they were later given their freedom. (According to the Taliban's interpretation of Islamic law, if you survive such a punishment, you're free to go.)

After the Herat executions, the official Taliban Radio Voice of Shari'a, clearly intent on sending a message to would-be sexual deviants throughout the land, proudly announced the heinous accomplishment: "Shari'a-prescribed punishment has been administered to two sodomites [in] Herat Province. The cases of the accused were investigated by the public prosecution office of Herat Province, where the accused confessed to their crimes without duress or torture."

The Taliban's treatment of homosexuality is pretty frightening stuff. But even scarier is that many of the countries being approached to join the United States in the fight against the Taliban don't treat homosexuals, and other citizens deemed second-class, in a drastically different way. Islamic fundamentalists and their fascistic beliefs have a grip, in varying degrees, on the leadership of many Muslim countries.

The Taliban offer what is perhaps the most extreme manifestation of discrimination against women. As has been reported in the media, women in Afghanistan are beaten to death, according to Amnesty International, for walking in public with a man who is not a relative. Women are also beaten and executed for walking alone at night, or having their ankles or wrists exposed.

The Taliban's brand of cruelty, garnering world attention in the wake of the World Trade Center destruction and the killing of almost 3,000 people, is perhaps enough to make some American gay activists and feminists hawkish, ready to blow the Taliban and Osama bin Laden to kingdom come.

"We have to go out and eliminate the threat or at least

significantly diminish it," says Washington, D.C., gay activist John Aravosis, who spearheaded the campaign against the antigay radio talk-show host Dr. Laura. "We have to destroy the people who launched this attack [on New York and Washington]. That means military action."

The many gays and feminists involved in the antiwar protests notwithstanding, Aravosis believes that gays and lesbians may be even more red, white, and blue than others right now.

"The gay businesses had the most flags up by far," he notes of shops in Washington, D.C., the day after the Pentagon attack. "I think we're just like everybody else, but to some degree I feel there's even a little more patriotism. Gay people are forced to understand the freedoms that we do or don't have as Americans. It requires you to think about the rights you're fighting for."

The Taliban's treatment of homosexuality isn't the main reason Aravosis believes military action is necessary—it is the attack on the Word Trade Center, he says, that warrants a response—but the Taliban's death penalty for homosexuality has made him increasingly comfortable with his position. "I would not shed a tear if that government should be destroyed or overthrown," he says.

On an emotional level, it's hard to disagree with Aravosis. Taking action, however, is far from cut-and-dried. Aside from the arguments of antiwar activists that torpedoes and ground troops will result in the killing of many civilians—including many of the women, homosexuals, and others being persecuted by the Taliban—the emerging coalition against terrorism is putting the United States in bed with several other dictatorial regimes that also subvert the rights of women, gays, lesbians, and transgendered people.

"I think we have to look at all the potential consequences to the coalition that the United States is trying to build, and the way it's building it," warns Surina Khan, executive director of the International Lesbian and Gay Human Rights Commission (ILGHRC). Born in Pakistan and raised in an Islamic family, Khan is more than familiar with the policies of some of the hard-line Islamic countries the United States has bolstered and whose abuses the U.S. has excused. While much of the Muslim world has condemned the terror attacks, views Islamic terrorists and regimes like the Taliban as having twisted the tenets of Islam, and may be more moderate toward women, on the issue of homosexuality Islam is fairly uniform across the board, as is much of Christianity. "Homophobia runs through mainstream, conservative, and fundamentalist elements of Islam," says Khan. "It's a common thread that runs through every Muslim nation."

George W. Bush has set the terms of the impending battle: the good people of the world against the "evil folks," making it appear as if every nation in the coalition against terrorism— including the United States—is a bastion of human rights, while Afghanistan's Taliban and any other country that doesn't join the coalition are the planet's only torturers, murderers, and supporters of terrorism. This administration, which hasn't exactly defined itself in its first ten months as one concerned about social issues in the United States, let alone abroad, is even suddenly talking about the Taliban's treatment of women, just as the rabidly conservative *New York Post*—no friend of the gay-rights movement—ran a few paragraphs in the aftermath of the attacks about the horrendously antigay policies of the Taliban.

The fact is, some of the countries the United States is now cozying up to have oppressive laws and policies frighteningly similar to the Taliban's. In Pakistan, the United State's newest ally in the so-called war on terror, homosexual acts between men or women are crimes punishable by death. Though the law is rarely enforced, it is used as a threat to intimidate people and as a blackmail tool by the police. In Kuwait, Bahrain, and Qatar, laws against homosexual acts are enforced with prison sentences of three to ten years. In the United Arab Emirates and Yemen, both male homosexuality and lesbianism are crimes punishable by death.

Women in Saudi Arabia are not allowed to drive, must get written permission from a male relative if they want to leave the country, and cannot walk outside without being accompanied by a male relative. Male homosexuality in Saudi Arabia is punishable by death. In 1996 a man was reportedly beheaded as a punishment for homosexuality. Last year, nine transvestites were subjected to 2,600 lashes each in public for performing "deviant" sexual acts, violating a UN convention Saudi Arabia signed that prohibits torture, and were sentenced to several years in prison as well. (Police had caught the men on surveillance cameras dressing in women's clothes.)

In Egypt, women run the risk of losing their citizenship if they marry a non-Egyptian. And fifty-two men accused of "practicing debauchery with men" have been on trial in Cairo over the past several months in a spectacle that has received international attention. The two main defendants have been charged with "forming a group that aims to exploit the Islamic religion to propagate extremist ideas."

The men had been arrested inside and outside a riverboat disco, the Queen Boat, that was raided last May. "This disco had a policy of admitting single people—most places admit only couples," says Scott Long, ILGHRC's program director. "The police targeted men who they thought were effeminate or men who were alone."

The arrests are part of what appears to be a crackdown by the Hosni Mubarak government that some believe is an attempt to distract Egyptians from the serious problems plaguing the country, while also pandering to Islamic fundamentalists by suppressing an increasingly visible gay community. A month before the disco raid, in April, reports emerged of men having been entrapped by police on the Internet as well: Posing as potential sexual partners, police met with men who were seeking sex online and then interrogated them, a tactic similar to the crackdowns on supposed pedophiles in the United States. A month earlier, an Egyptian computer engineer was sentenced to three years in jail, and an accountant to fifteen months, for engaging in the scandalous act of advertising for sex on the Internet.

Some of the Cairo 52 have reportedly been tortured and abused in jail, coerced to confess by use of electric shock treatment, and are being tried in State Emergency Security Court, a special court system that was created specifically to deal with terrorists and criminals who pose threats to national security. A fifteen-year-old boy who was swept up in the raid at the Queen Boat has already been tried, found guilty, and sentenced to the maximum penalty of three years in prison. The court ruled that he was guilty after a medical examination had showed he'd engaged in "debauchery."

The trial of the Cairo 52 resumes this month. There are fears among activists that Mubarak's government, wanting to appease angry Islamic fundamentalists while it sides with the United States against the Taliban and bin Laden, has cracked down even further on suspected homosexuals and that the fate of the Cairo 52 will be worse than previously thought.

"The 'war on terrorism' is seen in parts of the Middle East as an attack on Islam," Khan explains. "The government of Egypt, trying to appease the religious right's opposition to Egypt's participation in such a war," is ready to step up discrimination against homosexuals. Long adds that reports are surfacing of additional arrests. "I just got a note from Aswan saying a number of men were arrested in their flats," he says.

In August, Congressman Barney Frank and thirty-four other members of Congress sent a letter of protest to the Mubarak government, as have UN officials. But while activists say the state department under the Clinton administration was more vocally proactive on antigay human rights abuses around the world, prior to September 11 there was no pressure on Egypt by the Bush administration, and it's doubtful there will be any now.

It's understandable that the United States needs Egypt as an ally in isolating the Taliban; it's not in our best interest if Egypt experiences internal strife that might destabilize its government at this critical time. But the United States most certainly can— and must—speak up about Egypt's and other countries' human-rights abuses at the same time that it forms a coalition against terror. What, after all, is the United States fighting for when it claims to be preserving freedom and democracy?

"Egypt is already an ally—it's more than an ally, it's basically a client state of the United States," notes Long, referring to the fact that Egypt is the second largest recipient of U.S. foreign aid (Israel being the first). "We fund the Egyptian government, and that's why Egypt is joining the coalition. If we're going to use that relationship to engage with them on terrorism, we should not be afraid to use it to engage with them on human rights. These are fifty-two human beings. They range from young students to engineers to doctors to lawyers to construction workers, and they're facing persecution. They should not be further victims of September 11."

Village Voice, **October 3, 2001**

THE MOHAMED ATTA FILES

WITHIN DAYS OF SEPTEMBER 11, a rumor began wafting through media circles: Law enforcement was actively pursuing a theory that Mohamed Atta, the suspected ringleader of the September 11 hijackings and the pilot of the first plane to crash into the World Trade Center, was a homosexual.

Investigators have never confirmed the line of inquiry. Yet that hasn't stopped the speculation: "World Trade Center terrorist Mohamed Atta and several of his bloody henchman led secret gay lives for years," reported the *National Enquirer* in its November 6 issue. It's enough to make many a gay man or lesbian seethe with rage.

This line of thinking brings back painful memories of sensational media stories that have time and again equated gay with evil—from the serial killer Jeffrey Dahmer to the Gianni Versace murderer Andrew Cunanan. The latest is a new book by a German scholar that claims that Adolf Hitler was gay.

What, after all, should it matter to the FBI if Atta were gay? The fear is that such a line of inquiry seeks to establish, willfully or not, that murderous homosexuals—perhaps an entire network of them—are behind the terrorist attacks.

As outlandish as the Atta speculations may sound, it's the kind of narrative we've seen all too often in America. From the McCarthy era purges of homosexuals throughout the govern-ment in the 1950s, to the investigations into the assassination of President Kennedy (think Joe Pesci and Kevin Bacon in Oliver Stone's *JFK*), the notion of a dangerous homosexual conspiracy has reared its ugly head over and over again.

What is perhaps most galling about the subject right now is that while there may be a keen interest in proving that the enemy was homosexual, there has been much less interest in showing the heroes and victims of the attacks in the same light. In much of the media coverage since September 11, gays and lesbians have been made invisible among the victims of the attacks while heterosexual victims have been focused on with great intensity. A *Dateline NBC* segment that featured Mark Bingham, the rugby player who was among the heroes on United Flight 93 (which crashed into a Pennsylvania field after several passengers overtook the hijackers), omitted the fact that Bingham was openly gay, proud, accepted by his family, and left a grieving partner behind. But the program delved deep into the personal lives of the other heroes on the flight.

And yet, the desire to paint the enemy as gay seems to be quite strong. Two weeks ago, the Associated Press ran a photo of a U.S. Navy officer standing next to a bomb about to be dropped on Afghanistan on which somebody had scrawled HIGH JACK [*sic*] THIS, FAGS. That the photo got through the scrupulous military censors and that the AP chose to run the photo without commenting on the slur was yet another indicator of an impulse, unconscious as it might be, to paint homosexuals as villains in the national psyche. (Responding to angry complaints by gay groups, the U.S. Navy later apologized, as did the AP, saying it had made a "journalistic error.") In frightening times, there are always scapegoats, and gays are certainly an old standby.

That's what makes the inquiries into Atta's sexuality all the more dubious. Ironically, bells went off for many gay people themselves who read the *New York Times* interview with Atta's father. In it, the elder Atta talked of his son as incapable of hijacking a plane because he just wasn't man enough. "Toughen up, boy!" the father said he used to tell his son. (*Harper's* later noted that the father described his son as "girlish.") That's certainly a father-son relationship many gay men know intimately. The father also railed in the interview against the moral depravity of the United States, specifically singling out "homosexual marriages." And let's not forget the subsequent story in which it was revealed that Atta, who has been portrayed as hostile toward women, wrote in his will that he didn't want women near his body after his death.

But gay people also know that these indicators more often than not are stereotypes that are all wrong—there are plenty of macho gays, like the rugby player on Flight 93, and there are plenty of straight men who are gentle aesthetes who have sour relationships with their more manly dads. For those speculating about Atta's sexuality, there had better be a lot more to go on than these superficialities. And they'd better answer the most pertinent question their line of inquiry raises: Why does it matter?

Newsweek.com, November 2001

VIRTUALLY RECKLESS: THE CONTRADICTORY FACES OF ANDREW SULLIVAN

IN 1994 I WROTE a column in *Out* magazine, an abridged version of which was later reprinted on the op-ed page of the *New York Times* and which also prompted a *60 Minutes* segment. In the column, I discussed how I'd met a man in a bar and went home with him that night. We'd both had a few drinks, and in the heat of the moment, he didn't put on a condom before we had sex, and I didn't demand that he do so.

I reflected in the column on some of the things that fed into such a critical, momentary lapse for myself and, according to studies current at that time, many other gay men. I also discussed what we might do to guard against compromising ourselves in the future. Since then, I've written several pieces about gay men and HIV prevention, and covered the issue a great deal in my 1997 book, *Life Outside.*

One phenomenon I was not happy to be among the first to report on, in a column in *Out* in 1997, was that of "bareback" sex—a name given to it by its practitioners, gay men who had concluded from the new combination-drug therapies (and the media coverage that sensationally touted them as a virtual cure) that the AIDS epidemic was no longer a threat and had thus decided to forgo condoms entirely. For barebackers, unprotected sex is not a slip-up in the heat of the moment, but a firm decision to give up on protection, whether they are HIV-positive or HIV-negative. I came under tremendous attack for that column from various quarters. Some charged that it was sensational, that I'd focused on a small group of men who were far from the mainstream, though at the time a check of screen names on America Online alone showed an unlimited number of men advertising for bareback sex. Others charged that unprotected anal sex was mostly occurring among men who were HIV-negative and in monogamous relationships, but many of the men I interviewed were either in open relationships or were single and engaging in multiple-partner sex. Far too often, their HIV status was not the same as their sexual partners'.

Looking back, not only have the critics, sadly, been proven dead wrong, but I was reporting only the tip of the iceberg: bareback chat rooms and Web sites have sprung up all over the Internet during the past five years, and studies have shown remarkably high rates of unsafe sex among gay men. Depressingly, but not surprisingly, the latest reports have also shown rising infection rates for HIV Data available from New York City shows the incidence of new infections among gay men rose to 8.4 percent by 1999. In San Francisco, the incidence rate nearly tripled, from 1.3 percent in 1997 to 3.6 percent in 1999. Even as combination therapies are lowering viral loads and thus the infectiousness of those taking them, the sheer amount of unprotected sex now occurring is fueling rising rates of infection, and the AIDS epidemic among gay men continues to expand rather than contract. And combination therapies are failing many, and also showing long-term dangerous side effects.

Given everything I've witnessed about the rise of barebacking in the past several years, I could not help but be taken aback by a story I became privy to that has lit up the Internet over the past several weeks. The same was apparently true for many others, because it was the hot topic of discussion on message boards, from the gossipy gay site Datalounge.com to the gay conservative site Independent Gay Forum, from the often-liberal Salon.com to the rabidly right-wing FreeRepublic.com. The HIV-positive gay writer and pundit Andrew Sullivan, the information contended, had an assumed screen name on America Online with a profile that advertised for "bareback" sex and which linked to two Web pages where he posted headless photos and his sexual tastes, one of which was on BarebackCity.com.

Beyond the sensationalism of the "bareback" sex revelation, what was most jarring to people who'd received this information was the sheer incongruity between the public persona that many rightly or wrongly perceive as Sullivan's—conservative, moral, devoutly Catholic, marriage-minded, judgmental toward the sexual behavior of politicians and other public figures, and arrogant toward the ghettoized gay scene—and the person depicted on the sites, a gay stereotype more extreme than any of the Village People, someone very much in the gay sexual fast lane, all pumped up and describing his "power glutes," ravenously eager to hook up, but letting prospective partners know that "no fats, no fems" need apply.

The information about the sites was easy enough for any journalist to confirm early on. I did, eventually speaking with two men to whom Sullivan had identified himself through the screen name, one of whom met with him. I'd actually been informed about the sites days before the information had been posted on the Internet message boards; the information came from a source I've known and trusted for many years, a health-care professional. The screen name and the Web sites were shut down soon after the story was posted on the Internet.

According to several individuals at the *New York Times,* Sullivan acknowledged the existence of the sites and their exposure to at least one of his editors as soon as the information broke on the Internet (though he apparently kept out the major detail: that it was "bareback" sex that he was seeking.) Rather than deny the story outright if indeed it were a false, vicious rumor, Sullivan, who normally gives a comment to any reporter who calls him—and who has chided other public figures for not coming forward with the truth in such matters—has refused to respond to inquiries from a great many reporters, myself included. Silence has been golden in that regard: Except for a squib on Datalounge.com, commentary from Gaybc.com radio host John McMullen, and an item by *Village Voice* columnist Michael Musto, no mainstream or gay media have dared to go near this story.

And yet, it is a story that will not die. The message boards continue to be fired up, and it has made the e-mail rounds among media people, gay activists, and political operatives of all persuasions countless times. For many in the gay community, this an intensely important story that cuts across several issues of concern, from HIV prevention to the relationship between the pronouncements made by a gay public figure and his actions. Andrew Sullivan, who is the former editor in chief at the influential Washington weekly the *New Republic* (where he is now a senior editor, writing a regular column), and is a contributing writer to the *New York Times Magazine,* has a great deal of impact on the reporting of gay and AIDS issues.

It's true that for some who despise Sullivan for his political views, this may also be an opportunity to damage him. No doubt Sullivan supporters will say that about anybody who believes the story should be covered. I should point out that Sullivan and I have publicly and privately criticized one another's work, sometimes angrily, as we've been at odds on many issues since the early 1990s. Only two weeks ago I criticized him in my column on Gay.com, discussing something he'd written on his Web site, andrewsullivan.com.

That said, it is also true that Sullivan and I, like many writers and commentators, have been critical of one another precisely because of our differences over ideas—ideas that this particular story intersects and underscores. Deciding not to write and report on an important topic about someone with whom I have had some differences simply because it might appear personal would be shirking responsibility. While this story, like many others, involves issues of privacy and what the media should or should not report, to write off this discussion as nothing more than a baseless attack on Sullivan from his enemies on the left would be to dismiss it far too easily.

A COMPLICATED MAN

Andrew Sullivan is a bit more complicated than some of his harshest critics describe him. That's probably true of any author and commentator, but in Sullivan's case, many of his critics attack him based on his earlier writings, or even based on what others might say about him—i.e., calling him a "moralist" regarding gay culture—without taking note of changes he seems to have experienced and which were on display in self-revelations made in his second book, *Love Undetectable,* a beautifully written collection of essays on sex, love, and friendship.

Sullivan doesn't make it any easier for those particular critics, either. He redefines himself and revises his positions as he goes, often subtly moving away from positions that might have seemed too hard-edged or too definable, and he doesn't cop to it when he's changed a position.

That is particularly true when Sullivan takes up a point of view he once attacked, particularly those held by the many gay activists and writers he's lambasted in years past. On a wide range of issues, from his positions about the effectiveness of direct-action groups such as ACT UP to his positions about public figures' reluctance to acknowledge their sexual orientation if they are gay or lesbian, Sullivan has often done an about-face but makes it appear as if he's always been there, thus never admitting that he'd earlier derided others for the same positions. The public's attention span is short enough in the media age that Sullivan can get away with this virtually unscathed. Besides, even if called on it he can offer a nuance that he believes makes the position his own.

This habit of Sullivan's is less about his reluctance to be generous to gay activists, whom he remains quite hostile toward, and more about his now highly predictable quest to be viewed as an unpredictable contrarian. How, after all, can you be the contrarian with the "new" position that no one else has had while at the same time admitting it is someone else's idea you're now recycling?

Sullivan clearly goes to great pains to make himself indefinable, pointing to passages in his work that will exonerate him from this or that charge from any particular camp, but he nonetheless has taken some very definitive positions about his own behavior and that of others, the kinds of positions that stick in people's minds, his nuances and elusiveness notwithstanding. And this is where his critics' harshest charges are not off base.

As I've thought about his AOL sex profile and bareback-sex page during the past two weeks, two statements of Sullivan's stick out most vividly in my own mind. One was on the occasion of Sullivan announcing that he is HIV-positive, in an interview in the *Washington Post* in 1996. He became infected with HIV through an "accident," he said, not through "reckless" behavior. It was a statement that conjured up the idea of "innocent victims of AIDS," a term that Catholic AIDS groups and others have put forth to describe those such as babies who became infected while in their mothers' wombs and those who contracted the virus via a blood transfusion, as opposed to the guilty, sex-crazed homosexuals. Later, Sullivan explained what he meant by having an "accident" as opposed to being "reckless," stating that he contracted HIV via oral sex, rather than through unprotected anal sex.

Though the risk of contracting HIV through oral sex is far lower than through unprotected anal sex (which some might view as more irresponsible, and thus might be more embarrassing to admit), most people took Sullivan at his word, and many HIV-positive people were happy enough to have another powerful spokesperson. In fact, earlier Sullivan had focused public attention on the possibility of oral-sex transmission with his pronouncement, "I think the most important decision for gay men to make in 1995 is whether to have oral sex without a condom. . . . It's the issue of whether someone is killing someone or not."

The other statement of Sullivan's that boldly stands out to me in light of his bareback-sex page is about Bill Clinton and his sexual affair with Monica Lewinsky. Only a couple of months ago in his column in *The New Republic,* Sullivan lambasted Clinton for what he saw as the former president's "reckless, oblivious, careening narcissism," and then attacked him for his "sexual risks," which Sullivan also termed "reckless."

Recklessness has obviously loomed large in Sullivan's mind when it comes to sex. So do words like "pathological," as in his criticism of gay culture for its "libidinal pathology." Sullivan eloquently discusses his own sexual indulgences in *Love Undetectable,* and even defends them using recycled arguments made by gay sex radicals of the past—though, of course, he doesn't credit them (and later attacks them once again). His sexual behavior during the AIDS epidemic was "an unrepentant assertion of freedom, an assertion that the deepest personal struggles do not end in the middle of a crisis. Indeed," he writes, "in the middle of a crisis, refusal to end them is a mark of the ultimate resistance."

Even as Sullivan backs up and promotes his statements that marriage for gays is "the deepest means for the liberation of homosexuals, providing them with the only avenue for sexual and emotional development that can integrate them as equal human beings and remove from them the hideous historic option of choosing between their joy and their dignity," he defends his own sexual adventures in *Love Undetectable,* "marveling at the exotic beauty of other men, at the literally unbelievable sense of having them," and he discusses how "liberated" he feels in these sexual activities. Sullivan even discusses having had unprotected sex with another HIV-positive individual, an old friend, reveling in having "the barrier broke[n] at last." Still, he attacks the "gay liberationists" for the "tragic lie" they've promulgated, and he homes in on the "sexual pathologies that plague homosexuals." These conflicting arguments are not presented in any linear form; Sullivan shuttles between them seamlessly.

This may seem tortured and extraordinarily contradictory, but the logic that Sullivan is banking on is this: because of the ingrained homophobia that was present during his upbringing, he and his generation may be resigned to promiscuity, to choosing their "joy" over their "dignity," and may be a lost cause when it comes to relationships and commitment—which of course ignores the many gay men his age and older who are doing just fine in relationships, monogamous and nonmonogamous alike—but he's fighting for same-sex marriage for the next generation, so that they can live a different way.

It's a classic "do as I say, not as I do," argument. Whatever you think of his logic and analysis, he clearly cuts himself a lot of slack for his own indulgences, for succumbing to weaknesses, as Christians might put it. His own sexual behavior is "complicated," he says, and as in his statements of how he became infected with HIV, he doesn't dream of calling it "reckless." And yet, as in his broadsides against Clinton, he hurls the word "reckless" at others in merciless attacks.

These attacks lately have been part of an overall judgmentalism that has pervaded Sullivan's work, particularly on his Web site and on the more circuslike cable talk shows in the past year. He has railed against gay activists with more intensity than ever, talking of how he's "embarrassed" by them, comparing them in their zeal to the horrendously antigay Reverend Fred Phelps of Kansas who has brought his "God Hates Fags" signs to such events as Matthew Shepard's funeral. Sullivan has excoriated the "neo-Stalinists who run San Francisco," jabbed at the drug-addicted actor Robert Downey, Jr. and his "army of enablers," attacked "lunatic AIDS activism," opined that Al Gore "is a danger to the country and the Constitution," and stated that Bill Clinton is "not psychologically healthy" and should "see a shrink."

In a particularly gratuitous slam, Sullivan only a few weeks ago on his Web site described San Francisco's gay community as "frozen in time," unlike gays in the rest of the United States who are "increasingly suburban, mainstream, assimilable." "Here in the belly of the beast," he wrote in a swipe, "Village People look-alikes predominate, and sex is still central to the culture," as if his own bareback Web page doesn't evoke these very same stereotypes.

SULLIVAN V. SCIENCE

Among Sullivan's nastiest smears, however, have been his excoriations in the past year of AIDS researchers for having the audacity to release studies showing an alarming rise in both unsafe sex and infection rates of HIV among gay men in the United States.

For background, it's important to remember Sullivan's 1996 "When Plagues End" cover story in the *New York Times Magazine* which posited that AIDS, as a health crisis, had ended because of the onset of the drug cocktails that included the new protease inhibitors. People's lives had changed dramatically, he explained, and this should be acknowledged and celebrated. But while the lives of many mostly white, middle-class gay men had indeed been brought back from the brink by the triple combination therapies, many people rightly felt that several aspects of the article, and its overall message that the AIDS crisis in America was over, were vastly overstated and premature—and all of the latest studies, showing the increasing failure of the drugs as well as their long-term side effects (including heart and liver disease and possibly cancer), and showing rising infection rates among young gay men, bear this out.

Tragically, the article was enormously influential in pushing much of the rest of the media to focus on AIDS as under control.

In the years following, what was already a breakdown in safer sex among gay men only accelerated as more and more studies showed many younger gay men believing that indeed AIDS is no longer a threat.

Since that time, Sullivan has been on a mad tear, seemingly doing whatever he can to prove that all of the latest alarming studies are absolutely, positively wrong. This takes on even more significance in light of the news regarding his bareback-sex page. Last December, on his Web site, Sullivan called the *New York Times* veteran science reporter Dr. Lawrence Altman "a truly terrible science writer" for reporting on studies released by San Francisco's Department of Health that showed a dramatic rise in HIV infection rates in that city, which has been a precursor for the rest of the country with regard to the HIV epidemic. Sullivan not only threw cold water on the study, aligning himself with and even promoting a small fringe of activists who are AIDS denialists (and including some who believe HIV does not cause AIDS), but he even claimed on his Web site that the agency had retracted the study.

"San Francisco's Dept. of Public Health later retracted their hysterical report, based on bad statistics, and conceded there was no evidence of a new epidemic," he stated. The agency did nothing of the kind—as it later told the *New York Post* and other news outlets—and actually released further data later in the year that confirmed the initial findings.

In Sullivan's world, anyone, including scientists who have been studying the epidemic tirelessly for the past twenty years—many gay men among them—who says that unsafe sex and infection rates are up are "doom-mongers." To him, all of the recent studies and subsequent media reports showing unsafe sex, HIV infection, and other sexually transmitted diseases among gay men are on the rise—reports that are now coming fast and furiously, from San Francisco, from Seattle, from New York, from Dallas, from Miami, from Chicago, from London—are part of some nefarious plot by "AIDS organizations eager to hit up donors for more money."

Recently, the Food and Drug Administration decided to rein in drug companies that were advertising protease inhibitors using models who are blond, muscled, gorgeous, and climbing mountains—making it seem as if you, too, could be that way if you took this or that drug to treat your HIV infection. The FDA's interest here was in making sure the companies were not engaged in false advertising to those infected with HIV, in terms of what the drugs would do for them, and what nasty side effects they could expect.

San Francisco's openly gay supervisor Tom Ammiano, however, in line with many HIV-prevention experts across the country, also saw a value in toning down the ads for the sake of those who are negative as well, as the ads fed into an overall glossing over of the realities of HIV infection, which studies show inhibits some younger gay men's will to remain safe. To Sullivan, however, the motives of Ammiano and others were immediately suspect. They were "truly bitter activists in SF [who] can't bear the sight of some people actually doing well on HIV meds." He then added: "The reason people might think unsafe sex is less risky today is not because they just saw an ad. It's because the risks of getting HIV today are far lower than they were just five, let alone ten, years ago." Of course Sullivan offered no evidence to back up such a remarkable claim.

Dr. Thomas Coates, director of the Center for AIDS Prevention Studies in San Francisco, says that five years ago, as well as ten years ago, infection rates and prevalence of HIV in the gay community are more likely to have been lower than now.

"People aren't reading the literature carefully enough," he

says. "You have to take into account the higher rate of [other] STDs—and a higher prevalence of other STDs makes infectious [HIV positive] people more infectious—and you have to take into account that more people may be in a primary HIV infection period [which also makes them more infectious], and that there are more people with HIV in general [because they are living longer]. The incidence rates are going up. So, the combination of things may counterbalance the fact that people are on medication [which may lower their infectiousness] and result in a situation where in fact it is just as easy to acquire or transmit HIV as it was five or ten years ago."

In his own defense of his bareback activities, as he has suggested, Sullivan might say that he is an HIV-positive man seeking bareback sex only with other HIV-positive men; some of his defenders on the Internet have already made this argument. This, of course, ignores the very real possibility of reinfection—or, as it's technically called, superinfection—with different strains of HIV and, more catastrophically, the rapid transmission of drug-resistant strains if so many people are having unprotected sex and passing on various strains of the virus.

"The phenomenon is absolutely true," says Coates, the San Francisco epidemiologist. "Superinfection does take place. That's been established looking at people in Africa and also looking at people who were infected through transfusions. The question that's unknown is how often this happens." Data from a study in Ottawa, Canada, last year confirmed that superinfection has occurred through sexual transmission between gay men.

Focusing on the question of reinfection assumes that Sullivan is engaging in bareback sex exclusively with other HIV-positive men. On his page on Barebackcity.com, where his name was "RawMuscleGlutes," Sullivan filled out a generic form that is on the site and which offers choices that are in the slang of the bareback underground. He checked off the various boxes: "I take loads in my ass. I take loads in my mouth. I give loads in asses. I give loads in mouths. My HIV status: Poz. I prefer you to be: Poz. I'm interested in bi scenes. One-on-ones. 3-ways. Groups/ Parties/Orgies. Gang Bangs."

In a space where Sullivan had an opportunity to write in his own preferences in his own words, he didn't write "seeking HIV positive only," as some other HIV-positive barebackers do on bareback sites. It's hard to imagine, too, that, though he says he "prefers" his partners to be HIV-positive, that Sullivan will find many HIV-positive women for the bi scenes and group scenes he is interested in.

One of the men who communicated with Sullivan under his sex screen name on AOL told me that Sullivan's profile on AOL did not previously state that he was HIV-positive. When he added his HIV status, he also added that he is a "healthy undetectable." Such a term, referring to his viral load, is not a cosmetic term, but a medical one that is often used as a proxy, though an imperfect one at best, for the infectiousness of an individual in terms of passing on the virus: That proxy might be used by HIV-positive men concerned with reinfection, but it might also be welcomed by HIV-negative men persuaded that their risk for HIV is thus eliminated.

The word "undetectable" has been overused and is deceptive, as if the person has no virus at all and is perhaps not infectious at all. Studies have found that while the virus might be "undetectable" in the blood, it can still be present in much higher levels in the semen. Also, viral load may fluctuate on a variety of factors, including adherence to medications, diet, and stress. Just because someone's viral load is found to be undetectable in his or her last test, which most people with HIV have performed no more than quarterly, doesn't mean it's that way at every moment.

CONFRONTING OURSELVES

It's hard to know how, if at all, Sullivan will respond to the issues raised by the revelation of his bareback-sex page. On andrewsullivan.com, he has acknowledged that he is perceived as a role model by some younger gay men.

"I do think a lot of young gay men do not practice safe sex, and a lot of it has to do with the fact that they didn't go through what a lot of the older generation went through with AIDS," says Corey Johnson, the nineteen-year-old activist who came to public attention when, as the captain of his Masconomet, Massachusetts, high school football team, he came out of the closet and was profiled on the cover of the *New York Times Magazine* last year. "They feel it can't happen to them," he says of gay men his own age. "I feel when people see that someone like Andrew Sullivan posts on BarebackCity.com, whether he's positive looking for other positives or not, I think it does do something to young people psychologically, where they think it's okay, and that they can't be hurt by it."

Sullivan would likely reject responsibility of this sort. But his denials of studies that show rising rates of infection are the kinds of ludicrous "ifs" and "buts" that anyone can say about any study when he or she truly doesn't want to believe its true. However, when the studies keep rolling in, and when the weight of the international science community is against you, it becomes increasingly difficult to discredit them. That is perhaps why Sullivan has restricted his attacks on AIDS researchers and journalists reporting on AIDS to the underground world of andrewsullivan.com, and hasn't yet brought them to the *New York Times Magazine*. There, he would come under strict review.

This is not the first time that mounting evidence overwhelmed the hope to believe otherwise. Back in the 1980s, when the AIDS epidemic first surfaced, gay men understandably had enormous problems absorbing the magnitude of what was happening. Many delayed and dawdled, tried to look the other way, and continued on with their lives as if nothing out of the ordinary was happening, while their friends were silently becoming infected and sick.

In many ways, that seems like a faraway, terrible time. But in other ways it seems reminiscent of that time right now, as many gay men of an entirely new generation are becoming infected while some of the people they might look up to are rationalizing away their own behavior, telling themselves that it's all some plot by others to deny us our freedom. Reality may sink in when we see that masses of gay men of newer generations are downing handfuls of powerful, near-toxic drugs each day, enduring ugly long-term and short-term side effects, and often seeing the drugs fail them entirely. And it will unmistakably sink in if the worst implications of drug-resistant HIV strains are realized, and many of these younger men begin to die.

In *Love Undetectable,* Sullivan himself is brutal toward gay men who were at the center of the early 1980s AIDS epidemic, lambasting their "knee-jerk defense of catastrophic destruction," accusing them of having "facilitated a world in which gay men literally killed each other by the thousands," having "rationalized away a communal bloodbath." In his own hyperbolic way of describing that generation, Sullivan actually gets at something that might explain why he, a man who has struggled with being what he believes is moral, may find it difficult—if not impossible—to admit that he has been wrong about the epidemic today, and about his own behavior.

"Once every gay man had been absolved from responsibility

for giving HIV to another man, then it was hard to go back and admit a mistake," Sullivan wrote. "Because the crimes of this regime were so enormous, and their consequences so grave, it became unimaginable to address, let alone confront, the moral responsibility they entailed."

LGNY, May 26, 2001

Note: Soon after the publication of this article, some media outlets reported on it while others—particularly those that maintained friendship or business ties to Sullivan—ignored the story. If only because of a typically sensational New York Post story—"Top Gay Columnists Go to War"—as well as furious debates about the story all over the Internet, Sullivan was forced to respond, lashing out at me on his Web site in an entry titled "Sexual McCarthyism." He defended his behavior as well as his views of HIV and its transmission. Several months later, however, when further studies showed the likelihood of superinfection among HIV-positive people having unprotected sex with one another, Sullivan wrote a piece in The Advocate admitting the possible consequences of his and others' actions. Nonetheless, his public contradictions and confused thinking have continued, most notably with his unabashed support of—and, later, his bitter anger at—George W. Bush and the Republican Party.

CRUISE (SPIN) CONTROL

HIGH-POWERED LAWYERS AND PUBLICISTS have always been at the core of Hollywood's power, making sure the big bucks keep rolling in. And since Hollywood is all about images that are packaged and sold, sometimes it's the lawyers' and publicists' job to promote a specific image—and other times it's their job to squash it.

Fearsome publicists like Pat Kingsley make sure that certain discussions about stars—Hollywood's glittering cash cows—do not get into print. As the MSNBC columnist Jeannette Walls described in an entire chapter of her 2000 book, *Dish* (William Morrow and Co.), one of Kingsley's tasks for years has been to make sure that magazine writers and other journalists do not ask Tom Cruise about the gay rumors surrounding him—often by threatening the magazines' editors from having access to other stars. For Hollywood's titans, having a discussion of the Cruise gay rumors—even if they are not true—would raise the issue of why Hollywood is so afraid of having openly gay leading men, and that's a discussion they do not want to broach.

Thus, the story of Cruise filing a defamation suit last week because of a report that he had a gay affair at least had the potential of underscoring Hollywood's queasiness about known gays in its midst and the lengths to which the industry will go to protect its stars. Not to mention that, as an extra, added bonus, it brought the rumors about Cruise to international attention and thrust them into the mainstream media once and for all. Some people even thought that there was a chance it would end with the rumors about Cruise being confirmed.

But the Hollywood machine is too well oiled for that: Cruise and company would not have proceeded with such a suit, elevating an obscure foreign report, unless they knew exactly where this would go. With the Cruise lawsuit, they indeed seem to have made sparkling California lemonade out of some pretty bad lemons. Now, the whole affair is starting to look like a remake of *The Talented Mr. Ripley*—yes, with perhaps yet another very confused homosexual at the core.

Cruise sued gay male porn star Kyle Bradford for $100 million for allegedly giving an interview to a French gossip magazine saying he'd had a sexual tryst with the actor. Cruise's lawyers denied that Cruise is gay and called such a characterization "vicious." The suit claimed that rumors of Cruise being gay could "cost Cruise very substantial sums" because of the macho roles he plays and the public's perceptions of him, implying of course that all homosexuals are mincing pansies, or at least that most people think that. Bradford denied that he gave the interview, in a brief statement on his Web site: "I have never been to France, I have never spoken with *Actustar* Magazine, and have never said any of the statements allegedly said by me."

It was not exactly a denial of knowing Cruise, however, and certainly kept the gossip columnists jumping for the next several days. Not to mention that Nicole Kidman, perhaps playing hardball in the divorce proceedings and trying to get as much as she can, refused to offer any comment to columnists looking for confirmation of Cruise's heterosexuality. Some reports pointed to Bradford's having spoken in the past to friends about knowing Cruise, and perhaps having given an interview to a different magazine, the information from which somehow made its way to *Actustar*. (*Actustar* has since printed a retraction and an apology.)

But this week *Village Voice* columnist Michael Musto interviewed Bradford's ex, and implied that Bradford (aka Chad Slater, aka Phil Navarone), if he did indeed tell people that he knew Cruise, was perhaps being a bit creative.

"I was with him almost a year, but I didn't really know him until after about six months," Randall Kohl told Musto.

"I noticed his lying when he said he was going to appear on [the British music show] *Top of the Pops* and he didn't—he actually went to Europe to wrestle. He said he did a Kentucky Fried Chicken commercial that I found out was not true."

Says Kohl: "He wants to be like Tom Cruise. Deep down, Chad thought he was Tom in his mind. He thought he looked a lot like him—he told me he did." Yes, shades of Matt Damon in *Mr. Ripley*. According to Kohl, before all of this, Bradford did give an interview about a supposed relationship with Cruise to the *London Daily Mail,* but it never ran, as the paper reportedly had doubts about it.

Now Bradford, obviously feeling the heat from lawyers, has

changed the statement on his Web site. It now refers to "the false and vicious stories that I had a gay sexual affair." Bradford says that he "doesn't know Tom Cruise and never said" that he did know him. "I haven't the slightest evidence of Tom Cruise being gay," Bradford states unequivocally. "I understand Mr. Cruise's anger over this article. It is disgusting. I am equally angry. If I can assist him in discovering the person or persons who started this completely false story, I will."

So, now we've gone from a story that might have unsheathed Hollywood's homophobia or at least provided us with some juicy gay dirt, to one that perhaps was created in the mind of an overzealous young man, to one in which that same young man, no doubt with a gun held to his head by shrewd Hollywood lawyers, is forced to describe a revelation of homosexuality as "vicious" and "disgusting."

Score another one for the Hollywood machine.

Gay.com, May 11, 2001

AIDS AT TWENTY: COMPLACENCY RETURNS

AS THE MEDIA MARK the twentieth anniversary of AIDS this week, those of us old enough to remember can't help but think back to 1981. And that, for me, sheds some light on why we're seeing a frightening rise in unsafe sex and HIV infection rates among young gay men today. Some people might see "AIDS at 20" as another media device—lots of news and feature packages to sell ads—but taking a moment to look back could be instructive as we head into a dangerous and uncertain stage in the epidemic.

Last Friday, the U.S. Centers for Disease Control and Prevention released a study that provided the most sweeping evidence yet of a return to a 1980s-era AIDS surge. New infection rates for gay men in the United States, between the ages of 23 and 29, have almost doubled from a few years ago, rising to 4.4 percent per year. In 1997, when the new infections were averaging between 2 and 2.5 percent per year, epidemiologists expressed great alarm, warning that if the number remained constant, in ten years, approximately 25 percent of gay men in that age group would become HIV positive.

Now, with the new figures, that would happen in a little more than five years, and in ten years, nearly half of that age group could be HIV positive. Now, what was considered an unacceptable rate three years ago—2.5 percent for all gay men—applies to white gay men alone, and among black gay men, the rate is more than 14 percent, a devastating number.

The new evidence of an AIDS surge—a second wave, as some have called it—may be staggering, but, for me, thinking back to 1981, it is almost understandable. Why I say "almost" is simply because we as a community should have learned from our mistakes. Tragically, we didn't. Many of us believed the hype about drug cocktails consisting of protease inhibitors being some sort of "cure." We reveled in the idea that maybe the epidemic was over. Of course, who could blame us for wanting an ounce of hope to mushroom after twenty years of madness? So, many of us went back to our lives as the epidemic receded from the spotlight. But now the complacency has taken its toll: The next generation seems to be going through precisely the same scenario that the previous one did.

That said, thinking back twenty years, it's understandable to me why many young gay men—and many older gay men—are having unsafe sex. I was in college from 1981 to the mid-1980s, not a care in the world. I remember hearing rumors of a disease among gays, or even seeing a report now and then. But I didn't pay much attention to it. I was just coming out, exploring my homosexuality, making the scene, cementing friendships, dating and, yes, having a lot of sex.

There was no overwhelming consensus about AIDS as a real threat in those early years—a least among a lot of men my age—and there was a lot of denial among many gay men of all ages. The media had hardly covered it. Slowly, the safer-sex message was being put forth by gay groups and gay activists. But I and many others my age—like many young gay men today—were not plugged in to activism, nor did we read the gay press.

Searching my mind now, I realize that even though I knew that AIDS existed and that condoms protected you, I was not using condoms in those early years, at least not all of the time. People my age—who were in their early twenties in the early 1980s—didn't think we were going to get infected. AIDS was something happening to older gay men, and it didn't seem so risky to have anal sex without condoms, particularly if it was only once in a while. For me, it was not until the enormous publicity surrounding Rock Hudson's death from AIDS in 1985 that I became jolted.

Sadly, in the media age, where celebrity is supreme, it took such a high-profile case to awaken me. That, coupled with the fact that the media seemed to come alive on the issue of AIDS soon afterward—finally reporting on AIDS daily and on the front pages—seemed to push me to become fully conscious. There's also nothing quite like seeing your friends wither away and die (and I began to lose quite a few) to make you see that something is real and deadly.

But it was the intense media coverage that influenced me to become vigilant about safer sex, even before my friends got sick and died. By the mid-to-late 1980s, the coverage was a constant reminder of the horrors of AIDS, and of its ever-present danger—even if it was often sensational. Since the onset of protease inhibitors in the 1990s, however, coverage of AIDS has slacked off dramatically. When the media has reported on AIDS, it's been focused on almost as a "manageable" illness. The drug regimens, the side effects of the drugs, and the failure of the drugs—as well as the spread of drug-resistant strains—all seem to have been played as a sort of sidebar, minor stories to the larger story of AIDS being under control. Not surprisingly, recent studies have shown that unsafe sex has risen dramatically among gay men because they see AIDS as less of a threat. In recent years, this has reached the point where unprotected sex has been glamorized, with "bareback" sex having become a dangerous trend.

This kind of throw-caution-to-the-winds attitude can only exist in a world in which AIDS just doesn't seem like a big deal—such as in the early 1980s. Today, many young gay men see AIDS as mostly vanquished and certainly controllable. That's why some of the reports in the big cover stories and TV news packages this week marking "AIDS at 20" are jolting many, young and old alike.

"Just a few years ago, there was hope that AIDS could be cured by aggressive deployment of the antiviral drugs," reported *Newsweek*'s David France in the magazine's "AIDS at 20" cover story. "Not anymore. Now research indicates that a patient would have to take the current medications for seventy years to eradicate the virus. It is increasingly obvious that few patients will tolerate long drug exposures without suffering disabling bouts of diarrhea or nausea, osteoporosis, pitch-black depression, diabetes or crippling pain in their hands or feet. Doctors say serious drug side effects will hamper nearly all the 450,000 Americans on AIDS medications. Liver cirrhosis . . . may soon become the leading cause of death for people with AIDS, experts say."

Marking the anniversary of a disease is pretty morbid, and

the whole idea is sickening to some. But if activists can use the media coverage—and expand upon it—to jump-start prevention efforts, "AIDS at 20" could be a turning point.

Gay.com, June 6, 2001

ANTIWAR AND OUT OF FOCUS

DESPITE THE FACT THAT protesters have organized successful marches in cities around the country, the current peace movement doesn't seem to be growing or garnering a real buzz on the street, even among many people on the left. Polls show that since September 11, since George W. Bush began talking about military action and since the peace protesters took to the streets, Americans are more—not less—supportive of military action. According to a recent Gallup poll, 90 percent of the public now believes bombing the Taliban is necessary.

Over the past few weeks I've spoken with quite a few people I'd have expected to be on the front lines of the peace movement, but who support the bombing campaign that has been under way, even if they do not passionately do so (and really, anyone passionate about possibly killing civilians—or anyone—would scare the daylights out of me). They may not be hanging out their flags, but they're certainly not burning them. So far, the antiwar message isn't permeating even its target audience.

Why the resistance to the resisters? Having run press and publicity operations for the media-savvy AIDS activist group ACT UP in the late 1980s, I speak from experience when I say: Ya gotta have a gimmick. Put less succinctly, in appealing to the public for support you have to have concrete and realistic goals, spelled out in a discernible and captivating message that will resonate with people once they are educated on the issues. With their hackneyed sound-bites—"Justice yes, war no!"—their noble but often untenable loyalty to pacifism at all costs (which some might call "fundamentalism" in and of itself), and their confusion about alternatives, the antiwar protesters don't appear to possess any of that.

Ironically, the antiwar activists' larger critique, percolating under the trite and nostalgic slogans, is on target and is even agreed upon by foreign-affairs specialists across the political spectrum—notwithstanding the cadre of right-wing pundits who have tried to portray the antiwar protesters as wing nuts and traitors. A logical solution to the current crisis is one that seems illogical and contradictory on the surface: give in to the terrorists' demands—and simultaneously hunt them down and destroy them. The antiwar protesters have had half of that right when speaker after speaker at their rallies has charged that U.S. policies in the Middle East have fomented outrage in the Islamic world and must change—even if, from a P.R. perspective, it's pretty callous to appear to be blaming the victim days after an horrific attack.

Al Qaeda's complaints, shared by millions of Muslims, are all about U.S. involvement in the Muslim world. Who could disagree? We have propped up dictatorships throughout the Arab world as we have simultaneously propped up Israel, while looking the other way as Israel has chased Palestinians from their homes and murdered many. Al Qaeda and other terrorist groups have exploited the anger against us among a fervently religious, politically disaffected swath of Muslims globally. And the millions of comparatively moderate Muslims across the globe who don't support terrorism or Islamic fundamentalism are often nonetheless indifferent or downright hostile in the face of the United States' current plight because of U.S. policies in the Middle East.

If the United States forced a settlement between Israel and the Palestinians by putting pressure on Israel as equally as it pressures the Palestinians—and strongly condemned and punished Israel for its human rights atrocities just as it condemns terrorism by Islamic fundamentalists—many Arabs across the world would see a different United States. They might even have more respect for democracy in time and beat back the fundamentalists among them rather than passively supporting their own dictatorial governments that, to varying degrees of success, keep the fundamentalists in line through brutal measures.

Where the peace movement is completely off the mark, however, is in demanding that no military action—and thus no strong response at all—come from the United States regarding the September 11 attacks. The terrorists must be punished for attacking our country, no matter how much their reasons for mass murder are couched in legitimate grievances. Ditto the governments that harbor and support them. Otherwise, any rogue state or crazed foreign group will believe it can easily get away with entering the United States and killing thousands of Americans at its whim.

This is where the antiwar people offer no realistic alternative and where their message is muddled. For example, some of the antiwar protesters have claimed that, rather than taking military action, we should bring the perpetrators to trial in an international court—as if it would be easy to just go and extract Osama bin Laden from Afghanistan and bring him to trial, convict him, and send him to prison. The protesters have often claimed that attacking the Taliban will only instigate further terrorist attacks—a "cycle" of violence. But taking bin Laden into custody—if that were even possible—could incite terrorism just the same, if not more. If bin Laden were in prison, many future terrorist attacks could conceivably be made, demanding bin Laden's release and threatening further action. Or Americans would be taken hostage with the condition of their release being bin Laden's freedom. We've seen these kinds of strategies countless times before among terrorist groups.

And even this, the only proposed alternative from the antiwar protesters—bringing bin Laden to trial—is not supported by a great many of them. "Some look to promoting international tribunals," says Andy Thayer, a Chicago antiwar activist and cofounder of the Chicago Anti-Bashing Network, a gay and lesbian group that opposes the current military action. "I'm personally extremely skeptical of this approach as the United States has made it clear that it wouldn't submit its own officials to such jurisdiction. . . . Without the United States also submitting to such a court (while insisting that foreign nationals be subject to it), it's just another case of the United States playing bully, and arrogantly insisting that a different standard be applied to it vis-à-vis the rest of the world." Thayer thus believes that the only response is to change our policies in the Middle East, end of discussion.

The antiwar movement in the Vietnam era grew over time

and resonated with millions because Americans increasingly felt they had no business micromanaging that part of the world, particularly if it meant many Americans would die in the process. Americans might be convinced in time that they have had no business, for the past several decades, micromanaging the Middle East either, and might work toward changing that now. But it will be difficult to convince substantial numbers of them that they shouldn't be responding swiftly and with force to the murderers who've killed thousands of people, or that the United States shouldn't be sending a message to other would-be terrorists. And unless the peace movement agrees upon and clearly lays out a realistic alternative, it will be impossible.

New York Press, **October 20, 2001**

TALES FROM THE DARK SIDE

WHILE READING DAVID BROCK'S illuminating and at times enraging new political memoir *Blinded by the Right: The Conscience of an Ex-Conservative,* one question kept flashing through my head: Why the hell didn't I out this guy?

There he was, a closeted gay right-wing journalist, working with such illustrious gay-bashers as religious zealots James Dobson and Pat Robertson, *Weekly Standard* editor Bill Kristol, then–*Washington Times* editor John Podhoretz, and *American Spectator* editor R. Emmett Tyrrell in the late 1980s and early 1990s. He was conspiring with them and many others against what they saw as the evils of liberalism. In the guise of journalism, Brock spun out, as he now describes it, a "witches' brew of fact, allegation, hearsay, speculation, opinion, and invective" about Anita Hill—the woman who'd accused Supreme Court Justice Clarence Thomas of sexual harassment during his Senate confirmation hearings—and, later, an equally toxic potion of often unsubstantiated allegations about President Clinton. All the while Brock secretly harbored a libido that was precisely of the kind that many of his coconspirators were railing against at that time.

Meanwhile, during roughly those same years, I was engaged in my own crusading and controversial journalism, revealing in columns and articles that publishing tycoon Malcolm Forbes, Hollywood mogul David Geffen, Assistant Secretary of Defense Pete Williams (in Bush the elder's Pentagon), and quite a few other public figures were secretly gay while they promoted homophobes or enforced antigay policies. Surely Brock should have been on my list, and his hypocrisy should have been exposed long before he'd written his infamous "Troopergate" Clinton hit piece in the *Spectator* (which launched the Paula Jones lawsuit), before he'd become so valuable to the right that they'd just accept him as another house homo rather than dump him because of an embarrassing exposure. Reading *Blinded,* I was sometimes as mad at myself as I was at Brock.

When I say that to Brock half-jokingly in an interview, he replies, "I'd have been outraged at the time—but I certainly deserved to be outed."

It's a response that goes a long way toward showing the sincerity of Brock's apology for his past recklessness, as well as the validity of the political conversion from right to left that he lucidly details in his book.

Truth be told, Brock hardly dated and kept his secret tightly hidden in the early years as he moved through conservative circles; he wasn't as sloppy as the closeted Pentagon officials and

Republican Hill staffers—and even some closeted members of Congress at the time—who socialized often in gay circles and even in gay establishments. Brock wanted fame and fortune so badly, and was so "self-loathing" and in search of validation, he says, that he'd do whatever it took. And as his secret became better known in the early 1990s, Brock then just came out himself—prodded by some right-wing colleagues' impressions of a critical Frank Rich column in 1994 that they claimed was sexually suggestive (though that was hardly the case).

As Brock describes it, at that point, after the runaway success of his first book, *The Real Anita Hill,* and other attention-getting articles in the *Spectator,* he was worth too much as a hired character assassin for his homosexuality to matter to his benefactors. It was only when Brock, in his second book, 1996's *The Seduction of Hillary Rodham,* offered a more balanced look at the First Lady—rather than a hit job connecting her to criminal activity, which many expected—that his patrons on the right began to abandon him. That book, he says, was the very beginning of his long journey away from the right.

Blinded discusses in detail the sleazy journalism of the *Spectator*—where Brock says no fact checker even existed to check the details in his distortion-filled stories—and the cult leader Reverend Sun Myung Moon's conservative *Washington Times*; the pack of manipulators close to Clarence Thomas who Brock says helped shape his Anita Hill book; the political operatives behind Paula Jones; the financier Richard Mellon Scaife, a major funder to the anti-Clinton campaigns; and the infamous Arkansas Project, which was the right-wing conspiracy Hillary Clinton was talking about. The basic facts of these stories have been confirmed over the years in books and articles by Joe Conason, Gene Lyons, Jane Mayer, Jill Abramson, Jeffrey Toobin and others. Brock now provides the intimate details.

The cast of hypocrites, vipers, and freaks doesn't get any more perverse than those in *Blinded*. There's the story about the often self-righteous media pundit Laura Ingraham—one of Brock's gaggle of "fag hags"—who, "in a drunken stupor, crawled . . . on her hands and knees," looking for Brock at a dance club. There's the truly demented pundit Ann Coulter, who, Brock writes, "seemed to live on nothing but Chardonnay and cigarettes." (Brock tells me that Coulter, another of his "fag hags," used to give him "ex-gay" literature, trying to "convert" him to heterosexuality.) Former Clarence Thomas aide and current radio talk-show host Armstrong Williams—who, you may recall, was sued by a male bodyguard a few years ago who claimed he was sexually harassed by Williams, a case that was settled out of court—appeared to have come on to him at Williams's apartment, writes Brock, while asking him whether he was "dominant or submissive in bed." (This is the same Armstrong Williams who wrote a column last week lambasting Rosie O'Donnell supporters for using children "to push alternative lifestyles into the mainstream.")

And there's the bit about Web gossip Matt Drudge, who has reveled in exposing Clinton's sexual affair with Monica Lewinsky, in addition to spinning out sexual innuendo, half-truths, and lies about others. Brock says he went on a date with Drudge (though Brock wasn't really interested in him) shortly after Brock and Ingraham cohosted a dinner party for Drudge in June 1997 to draw Drudge closer into the right-wing cabal. While at the gay dance club Rage in L.A., Brock writes, the jealous Drudge purposely stepped on the foot of a man dancing nearby who was flirting with Brock. A few weeks later, the heartsick Drudge sent Brock an e-mail saying that Ingraham was spreading the rumor that Brock and Drudge were "fuck buddies," opining that he should only be "so lucky." (Drudge was outed in MSNBC.com columnist Jeannette Walls's 2000 book *Dish*; in response, he denied that he was gay, though Walls had on-the-record quotes from former friends and alleged boyfriends.)

Some in the media understandably have raised the question of Brock's credibility, asking how anything he says can now be trusted, and a few have summarily dismissed him for that reason. But some of the media dismissals may be about something else: self-preservation. Certainly many reporters and editors would rather forget about those ugly times than reexamine their own roles in having furthered Brock's vicious tales. Many in the mainstream media are implicated in *Blinded*, including *Newsweek* reporter Michael Isikoff, who, Brock writes, "had passed on to me a handful of Clinton sex stories that he was not able to get past his editors in the hope that I would follow them up," presumably so that Isikoff could then write about them after Brock did. And who can forget the glowing reviews of *The Real Anita Hill,* including from the *New York Times*'s Christopher Lehmann-Haupt? By now admitting that the book was a pile of trash, Brock reveals what biased fools such respected reviewers were—particularly since many others saw the book for what it was at the time.

Some of the media's impulse to dismiss *Blinded* was even on display March 17, when the *Washington Post* had the gay conservative author Bruce Bawer review Brock's book. Predictably, Bawer slammed the book and mocked its author. After a number of complaints, the *Post*'s editors admitted that Bawer shouldn't have reviewed the book because he had been a writer at the *American Spectator* as well. The decision to use Bawer seemed to betray an attempt, conscious or not, to marginalize *Blinded* by serving up a review that was a less-than-serious sideshow—two queens, now political opposites, having a catfight—rather than to examine some of the disturbing issues and events that Brock's confessions now raise.

Some might say I believe Brock because I *want* to believe him. But actually, I'd been quite skeptical of Brock and his several-years-long conversion for some time, both to colleagues and in print; in 1998, I was strongly critical of him in a piece I wrote for the *New York Observer.* I still have some lingering doubts about his motivations, as I'm sure Brock hopes his confessions are as financially successful as his lies were. (Then again, who wouldn't?) But I'm glad that, unlike the notorious McCarthy sidekick Roy Cohn and many others, Brock isn't going to his death working for those who work against his own kind, taking all of the secrets with him. Instead, he's apologized, and he's written a convincing and highly instructive book.

New York Press, **March 2002**

ROME'S SEX SUMMIT

WHO'D HAVE THOUGHT THAT the pope would ever call an emergency meeting in Rome of the American cardinals to discuss the topic of sex? Sure, the issues that have forced the Vatican to make that extraordinary move, we've been told through much of the media, are pedophilia and sexual abuse. But under the surface it's also been—if not more so—about consensual sex: sex by supposedly celibate priests, and yes, often of the homosexual variety. By now everyone's heard about the swinging Father Shanley, a priest with a sexually abusive past who was shuffled around from archdiocese to archdiocese with Boston's Cardinal Law's blessings, only to head out to Palm Springs, where he opened up a clothing-optional gay resort spa, all while he got a check from the church.

(Church officials thought he was out there in the desert tending to his allergies.) Turns out he's been living for some time now with what appears to be a much younger boyfriend.

The Shanley case shines a bright light on an uncomfortable aspect of the crisis. The vast majority of the cases of abuse we've seen in the media over the past several months have been male-on-male, and not between priests and little boys, but between priests and teenagers; often the abuser has been gay-identified. Some conservatives—yes, admittedly, even including some among that loathsome bunch at the *National Review*—have been right when they have pointed out that many of these men thus are not pedophiles as much as they are simply gay men in the priesthood (which some observers have speculated could be up to 50 percent gay) who struggle like their straight counterparts to keep the celibacy vow, and who wind up looking for the easiest venue for sex. And defensive liberal and openly gay pundits have been too quick to dismiss that observation, fearful of where it might lead.

It's true that some conservatives—and the Vatican itself—have equated pedophilia with homosexuality, and have then scapegoated gays, blaming gay priests for the current troubles (including those who have remained celibate). It's a nasty charge that feeds the heinous and wrongheaded belief that homosexuality and pedophilia are one and the same. And I've been among those who've given the Vatican a whipping for implying as much. It is, however, valid to ask if all of these are in fact cases of pedophilic abuse, and to conclude that many are not. Not long ago, septuagenarian Bob Dole leered at Britney Spears in a Pepsi ad, and I doubt anyone would call him a pedophile, his Viagra obsession notwithstanding. Being attracted to adolescents, whatever your sexual orientation, is normal and fairly accepted, reflected most prominently in

Calvin Klein's use of seminaked adolescents to sell products not to that age group but to the age group just above it.

Of course, it is wrong for an adult, particularly someone in a position of authority, to force sex upon a young person (and it is against the law in many states to have even consensual sex with someone under eighteen), but that doesn't make the abuser a pedophile, something even I admittedly may have confused in the past. (Technically, sex with prepubescent children is called pedophilia, while sex with postpubescent minors is called ephebophilia.) It may simply be a case of someone who under any other circumstances would be seeking sexual intimacy with someone of his or her own age, but under the forced celibacy of the church takes what he can get—literally—and what comes most easily. And that, all too often, means making advances on teens in his care, people over whom a priest has authority, can force himself upon, and can demand silence from.

The issues with which the Church is grappling are thus much thornier than they appear. And as if they are not complicated and controversial enough, another element far in the background is that sex between priests and teens, as well as with other adults, is not always abusive either—something else that many liberal and openly gay pundits have not wanted to discuss (but which the case of Father Shanley, out partying it up in Palm Springs, also underscores). For every case of abuse of young people we've heard about, there are perhaps many more that we'll never read about, locked away in people's minds, never reported (or reported, but locked away in a church file somewhere). But for every case of abuse between an older teen and a member of the clergy, who knows how many cases there are of consensual sex between such teens and priests?

When I was seventeen, I had sex with a Catholic clergyman on Staten Island, a man in his twenties. He was not someone from my church (I met him at a flea market), so this was not someone in a position of authority over me. There was nothing abusive or coercive about it. In fact, I saw the incident as something exciting, as part of my own sexual evolution and growth as a teenager, discovering my sexuality—and I felt sorry for this poor soul, walled off in his self-imposed prison. I knew he was hungry for it and had limited options. And I knew he'd be easy to get. If anything, one could say that *I* was the one targeting *him*. Yes, some will say that kids can be very pushy, and that that doesn't absolve the adult in such a situation. But when we're talking about people just on the cusp of legal adulthood, it all gets pretty murky.

So these are the kinds of issues that lie just underneath the surface of the crisis that has brought the cardinals to Rome. And for that reason, though some of the cardinals have claimed these issues would be raised in Rome, the summit will actually have accomplished little with regard to a discussion of human sexuality. As we've seen in the American Church with regard to the sexual abuse cases for decades, the summit's intention has been to map out strategy to avoid public relations disasters for the Church itself, at best offering up a plan to work better with legal authorities in cases of abuse. There's no way that the cardinals or the pope will address any of the underlying red-hot issues anytime soon in a straightforward manner, let alone move for any concrete changes.

The Church conservatives' proposals for change—to become more rigid, crack down on gay priests or even ban them outright—are impractical, unworkable and retrograde, not to mention that they scapegoat a group that has served the Church well, and that such proposals would be met with much resistance. It's been said before but bears repeating: The only workable solution is to go the other way entirely; to open the priesthood up to women, to end celibacy, to allow gay and straight priests to be sexually active and to marry. We will likely not see those things in our lifetimes. So for now, and sadly for a long time to come, it will be business as usual no matter how many Vatican summits are held.

New York Press, **April 23, 2002**

CARDINAL SPELLMAN'S DARK LEGACY

TWO SUNDAYS AGO, THE rector at St. Patrick's Cathedral, Monsignor Eugene Clark, gave a homily that inspired the kind of PRIEST BLASTS GAYS headlines that New York's tabloids thrive on. Standing in for the embattled Cardinal Egan, the archdiocese's number-two man blamed the sex-abuse scandal on gays, railed against homosexuality as a "disorder" and said it was a "grave mistake" to allow gays into the priesthood.

It may have been another trial balloon as the Vatican desperately attempts to change the subject and scapegoat gays. Or it may simply have been further ineptitude on the part of the increasingly feeble Cardinal Egan, putting the wrong person at the pulpit while he scampered away to the Bronx amid the crisis. The New York archdiocese later distanced itself from—though didn't refute—Clark's comments, and a discombobulated Egan offered a bizarre nonresponse when asked in Rome about homosexuals in the priesthood: "I would just say this. The most important thing is to clean up the truth. And the truth is I have never said anything." (Egan seems just a bit too desperate not to be on the record saying "anything" about homosexuality, perhaps fearful that his position might be pointed to, for whatever reason, in the future.)

Whatever Clark's rant was meant to convey, it represents a dangerous path for the Catholic Church to embark upon, one that will only embolden media-savvy gay activists—and a press corps much less loyal to the church than in years past—to begin exposing the many twisted, personal sexual hypocrisies that envelop the increasingly tainted, lying bishops and cardinals who are running the Church.

Clark's deceptions included equating homosexuality with pedophilia, the ugly lie we've been hearing from the Vatican and the American cardinals, both before and during the sex-abuse summit. But the seventy-six-year-old Clark also engaged in a larger, less-defined but more powerful deception. In putting forth the idea that homosexuality is a "disorder," and that it is a "grave mistake" to ordain gay priests, he implied that only the lowly priests—the alleged child abusers among them—are afflicted with the so-called "disorder." He wouldn't, after all, accuse any bishops or cardinals themselves of having the "disorder," nor would he say that it was a "grave mistake" to have ordained them, would he?

Yet, among the several skeletons in gay-basher Clark's closet is that he in fact dutifully worked as secretary for one of the most notorious, powerful, and sexually voracious homosexuals in the American Catholic Church's history: the politically connected Francis Cardinal Spellman, known as "Franny" to assorted Broadway chorus boys and others, who was New York's cardinal from 1939 until his death in 1967.

The archconservative Spellman was the epitome of the self-loathing, closeted, evil queen, working with his good friend, the closeted gay McCarthy henchman Roy Cohn, to undermine liberalism in America during the 1950s' communist and homo-sexual witch-hunts. The Church has squelched Spellman's gay life quite successfully, most notably by pressuring the *New York Times* to don the drag of the censor back in the 1980s. The *Times* today may be out front exposing every little nasty detail in the Catholic Church's abuse scandal—a testament to both the more open discussion of such issues today and the Church's waning power in New York—but not even twenty years ago the *Times* was covering up Spellman's sexual secrets many years after his death, clearly fearful of the Church's revenge if the paper didn't fall in line. (During Spellman's reign and long afterward, all of New York's newspapers, in fact, cowered before the Catholic Church. On Spellman's orders, New York's depart-ment stores—owned largely by Catholics—pulled ads from the then-liberal *New York Post* in the 1950s after its publisher, Dorothy Schiff, wrote commentary critical of his right-wing positions; Schiff was forced to back down on her positions.)

In the original bound galleys of former *Wall Street Journal* reporter John Cooney's Spellman biography, *The American Pope*—published in 1984 by Times Books, which was then owned by the New York Times Co.—Spellman's gay life was recounted in four pages that included interviews with several notable individuals who knew Spellman as a closeted homo-sexual. Among Cooney's interview subjects was C. A. Tripp, the noted researcher affiliated with Dr. Alfred C. Kinsey of the Insti-tute for Sex Research, who shared information on Spellman regarding the prelate's homosexuality. In a telephone interview with Tripp last week, he told me that his information came from a Broadway dancer in the show *One Touch of Venus,* who had a relationship with Spellman back in the 1940s; the prelate would have his limousine pick up the dancer several nights a week and bring him back to his place. When the dancer once asked Spellman how he could get away with this, Tripp says Spellman answered, "Who would believe that?" The anecdote is also recounted in John Loughery's history of gay life in the twentieth century, *The Other Side of Silence.*

"In New York's clerical circles, Spellman's sex life was a source of profound embarrassment and shame to many priests," Cooney had written in the original manuscript of his book. When Mitchell Levitas, who was then the editor of the *New York Times Book Review,* received the manuscript for review, he realized it was a book that would make big news; he sent the book over to Arthur Gelb, who was then the managing editor of the *New York Times.* Gelb assigned reporter Ed McDowell to the story. McDowell interviewed Cooney, and went about interviewing others who were relevant to the story, including church officials.

The archdiocese, however, went ballistic when presented with the information, and became determined to keep it from being published. Chief among those orchestrating the cleansing of Spellman's past sex life was none other than the current gay-basher Monsignor Clark, who, in an interview with the *Times,* called the assertions "preposterous," commenting that "if you had any idea of [Spellman's] New England background" you'd realize these were "foolish" charges. (I guess there are no homosexuals north of Connecticut, right?) The church sent John Moore, the retired U.S. ambassador to Ireland and a close friend and confidant of several Church officials, to appeal to Sidney

Gruson, then vice chairman of the New York Times Co. "The Times was going to report that Cardinal Spellman was a homosexual," Moore later told journalist Eric Nadler, who wrote a piece for *Forum* about the ugly little cover-up, "and I was determined to stop it." Moore told Nadler that this was the "third or fourth" time he had appealed to the *Times* regarding a sensitive Church matter. "They've always done the right thing," he said.

As Cooney describes it, he was soon told by his editors at Times Books that his sourcing wasn't good enough, and that the four pages would have to be cut. He could keep a paragraph that alluded to the "rumors," but he would have to state that the rumors had been strongly contested by many people—even though, in his research, that had not truly been the case. The discussion of Spellman's homosexuality in the book was reduced to mere speculation, which was branded as irrelevant:

> For years rumors abounded about Cardinal Spellman being a homosexual. As a result, many felt—and continue to feel—that Spellman the public moralist may well have been a contradiction of the man of the flesh. Others within the Church and outside have steadfastly dismissed such claims. Finally, to make an absolute statement about Spellman's sexual activities is to invite an irresolvable debate and to deflect attention from his words and deeds.

The dutiful *Times* then had another former U.S. ambassador to Ireland and friend of the Church, William V. Shannon, review *The American Pope* for the *Book Review*. Shannon's review was scathing, attacking Cooney for even bringing the subject up at all: "Prurient interest in the sex lives of public figures serves no useful purpose."

A Jesuit priest wrote a letter to the *Book Review,* which was published a few weeks later:

> Cardinal Spellman's sex life does not matter, but [his] homosexuality does. . . . it matters to thousands of people whose jobs, relationships and whose very lives are threatened because of their sexuality, all the while being forced to view and eat the hypocrisy of their church. And it enrages people that church men and women can retain their jobs, hiding behind their clerical and religious statutes while their own people suffer persecution, disease and discrimination.

Sadly, the Jesuit's words still ring true today, almost twenty years later. While Spellman has been long dead, his legacy of hypocrisy lives on: there are closeted homosexuals—often condemning "sexual immorality" publicly while having gay sex privately—throughout the uppermost echelons of the church today. The gay movement in the past fifteen years has taken on the Hollywood closet and the Washington political closet, both with dramatic success—and both those institutions have P.R. operations far more sophisticated than the Vatican's antiquated machine, which can't even seem to get the aging cardinals to attend a press conference. The media these days also has a much greater appetite for exposing sexual hypocrisy, and is no longer cowed by the Catholic Church. Going down this treacherous road of increased gay-bashing and scapegoating, the Vatican perhaps doesn't realize what it may be unleashing upon itself. If I were a closeted bishop or cardinal in America, I would be very afraid.

New York Press, **April 30, 2002**

DON'T HIDE THE TRUTH ABOUT AIDS

MUCH OF THE AMERICAN press seemed to lurch back toward the early 1980s two weeks ago, while reporting on the death of the famed celebrity and fashion photographer Herb Ritts.

It was downright creepy to see a Reagan-era euphemism for AIDS pop up as the cause of Ritts' death in obituary after obituary: "complications from pneumonia." The *New York Times,* CNN, the *Los Angeles Times,* the Associated Press (in a story that ran in *Newsday* and many other papers), and other media organizations quoted Ritts's publicist, also identified as a friend, who used that term to describe what brought the openly gay photographer's life to an end at the age of fifty.

Soon enough it was revealed in the gay press (and since has

appeared only in a few gossip columns) that Ritts had, in fact, been HIV-positive for years. His immune system had been sufficiently weakened; HIV infection had left him unable to fight off the pneumonia.

In other words, Herb Ritts's death was an AIDS fatality And the ignorance of the truth surrounding it signals that, once again, this is a disease that dares not speak its name. And that silence has consequences.

The *New York Times* policy regarding obituaries—formulated in 1986, precisely because of the problems encountered in reporting on public figures who died of complications from AIDS—states that "the obituary of a newsworthy public personality, of any age, should reflect energetic reporting on the cause."

The Associated Press doesn't have an official policy, but advises reporters to exhaust every means available—including interviews with the deceased's friends and family, public records and statements by doctors—to determine the cause of a public figure's death.

But it doesn't appear that there was any kind of "energetic reporting" in this instance. Most mainstream-press reporters seemed to have spoken to only one individual—the publicist— and even then seemed to have followed a sort of "don't ask, don't tell" policy.

The *Advocate,* the national gay and lesbian newsmagazine, however, did ask. And, lo and behold, the very same publicist offered a fuller explanation: "Herb was HIV[-positive], but this particular pneumonia was not PCP [Pneumocystis pneumonia, a common opportunistic infection of AIDS]. But at the end of the day, his immune system was compromised." That statement perhaps prompted the *Washington Blade,* the gay weekly in the nation's capital, to rightly run with the headline GAY PHOTOGRAPHER HERB RITTS SUCCUMBS TO AIDS.

It's nice to know that small pockets of the gay community might now have the full story. But the fact remains: Millions of Americans, gay and straight, still haven't a clue about what took the life of the celebrity photographer who was himself a big supporter of AIDS causes.

This isn't just another example of incomplete or deceptive reporting. It's also a tragic omission at a time when study after study shows unsafe sex and new infections continuing to rise steeply among younger generations of gay men, often because the realities of AIDS are abstract to them—enough to allow them to take foolish risks.

They are often too young to remember the AIDS deaths of celebrities, like Rock Hudson in 1985, which jolted America and the world. Most young gay men also have not watched their own friends die, as was the case for gay men of previous generations. This is true even as many of these young men become infected with HIV themselves and stay quiet about their illness, going on the drug "cocktail," chained for the rest of their lives to powerful pharmaceuticals that often have horrific side effects.

Those drugs have thankfully saved many lives. Ironically, they've also driven AIDS back into the closet. The decline of AIDS awareness in the newsroom mirrors what has happened in society in general. No longer are many people with HIV walking around rail-thin and gaunt. Many even use testosterone as part of their therapy, building up their bodies and developing bulging biceps, often appearing more fit than their uninfected friends. AIDS becomes increasingly invisible, on the streets as well as in the media, even as HIV infection is an ever-present danger. And clearly, though American fatalities have decreased a great deal, HIV still kills.

That's why the story behind the death of Herb Ritts, a man

who photographed Hollywood icons and shot music videos for youth idols such as Jennifer Lopez and 'NSync, would go a long way.

That is, if anybody actually heard about it.

Newsday, **January 13, 2002**

ROSIE'S GAY GOSPEL

ONE AFTERNOON A FEW weeks ago, I received several e-mails stating that Rosie O'Donnell had called me a "moron" and had claimed that I was among the reasons that she'd not come out of the closet earlier. Crazy, I thought. Sounds like some nutty *National Enquirer* item.

I mean, the moron part, okay—Rosie certainly could have said that, and my criticisms of her may have inspired it, even warranted it. But little me, a mere moron of a columnist, is what was standing between big and powerful Rosie and the closet door all this time? Surely even Rosie, susceptible to all the self-delusions that most megacelebrities are susceptible to, would not say something so utterly ridiculous and think that anyone would actually believe it.

But hey, it was for real, as Rosie said that and more in an interview she did with columnist Paula Martinac on PlanetOut.com:

> Q. What do you make of gay journalist Michelangelo Signorile's assertion that it was your desire to silence your gay critics that made you come out?
> A. He is a moron. His idea of gay America consists of only those he deems worthy enough. I do not enjoy him, his point of view or his rhetoric. (He isn't even funny.) One reason I did not come out sooner, I didn't want anyone to associate me with Signorile in any way. Same goes for Musto.

Musto had been out front in offering fair criticism of Rosie's subterfuge for years, and he's gotten her back up several times. What Martinac was referring to in her question was a column I'd written here just last month in which I'd discussed the careful cross-promotional marketing of Rosie's coming out in the media. I noted what a great thing Rosie's coming out would be for the issue of gay adoption, but the part I'm sure Rosie remembers most was when I noted her less-than-honest past, in which she endlessly carried on to her Middle America TV audience about her supposed crush on Tom Cruise while never saying a word about famous women she might have crushes on. We heard ad nauseam about her kids, but nothing about her co-parent and partner.

That wouldn't be a big deal now if not for the fact that Rosie, amidst the terrific things she's doing in bringing attention to the issue of gay parenting, is still distorting that past—and lashing out at anyone who has pointed to her obfuscations.

Everyone, in coming out, is entitled to having lied. We've all been there, and nobody—in the gay community, at least—ever holds it against you. You explain it, people understand, and you then move on. But in the first few weeks after her much-heralded coming out, Rosie instead attempted to put forth the rather bizarre notion that she didn't ever really hide her sexual orientation and that her panting for Tom Cruise was never meant to convey that she actually liked him sexually. (She only meant she wanted him to mow her lawn, she says.)

Beyond that, amid her good deeds, Rosie's also let out some rather homophobic whoppers of late—e.g., saying she wouldn't want her children to be gay—the kinds of things that betray she's got some issues to deal with. And the gay public and much of the gay media have simply given a pass on these statements. There's something scary, though sadly understandable, that happens to the gay public—starved for validation and visibility—when a celebrity comes out. Suddenly, that celebrity becomes the queer Mother Teresa, someone who can do no wrong (though Christopher Hitchens has shown that even Mother Teresa was no saint). Rosie's done some great work, but that doesn't mean she's flawless. The gay media should be the place where a healthy, balanced discussion of her statements and actions takes place. Instead, too many in the gay media become starstruck sycophants.

Even smart people fall under the spell: the longtime gay press reporter Rex Wockner, swooning that "Rosie . . . has handled herself fabulously in recent weeks," buys Rosie's statement that she's never been discriminated against as a gay person because, he claims, he has experienced discrimination only five times. Earth to Rex, come in please: the reason Rosie may believe she's never experienced discrimination is because she was closeted all these years. Or do you really believe that Rosie would have been handed a daytime talk show and a multimillion-dollar contract had she uttered the "L" word previously and let it be known that she might do so on her show? (An aside to this: If Rosie hasn't experienced discrimination, isn't she contradicting herself when she says that she doesn't want her kids to be gay because it's a "tougher" life?)

Because she is fearful of simply admitting that she was in the closet to advance her career, Rosie is now creating scapegoats and diversions. First she was saying she was never really in the closet. Now she's saying that she was, but that Musto and I were keeping her there. I'm flattered that Rosie would think that I might have the kind of notoriety that people, when they hear that she is gay, would think all about me, but I'm just not self-deluded enough to believe that one.

And this whole idea of not wanting people to "associate" her with certain gay people reveals that Rosie still thinks there's something unseemly to being gay. Most illustrative of this was her interview with Bill O'Reilly on *The O'Reilly Factor* recently. When the bombastic O'Reilly asked about Ellen DeGeneres's "in-your-face" way of coming out, Rosie agreed with O'Reilly that it was "offensive."

Now, from what I recall of DeGeneres's coming out, she simply let it be known that she was a lesbian, let it be known that she was in love with the actress Anne Heche, and was (initially, at least) as happy and affectionate with Heche in public as many heterosexual celebrity couples are. In discussing a plea that DeGeneres once made to a then-closeted Rosie to "march on Washington" in honor of the slain Wyoming student Matthew Shepard, Rosie commented to O'Reilly that part of why she declined was because "my worldview was not so myopic that all I see is gay issues. My worldview revolves around children."

It seems that it's not I, as Rosie put it, whose "idea of gay America consists of only those [deemed] worthy enough."

This, in fact, appears to describe Rosie herself. Coming out in the way that DeGeneres did, just to be open about your life and to show your love and commitment to another human being publicly, is "offensive" to Rosie. Marching on Washington against antigay hate crimes is "myopic." But coming out with a "worldview" that "revolves around children" is the respectable way to come out.

Well, Rosie, I think it's great that you love children and want to adopt them. And I will support and fight for your right to do so. But please try to understand—try for a minute to think outside your own larger-than-life life—that for many others of us that's not the reason we came out. Many of us have a broad array of other issues and reasons—not the least of which is to simply live honestly—and none of them are "offensive." You don't want people to tell you the right way to be gay. That's fine. But don't tell us—and the rest of America—the right way to be gay either.

New York Press, **April 16, 2002**

Note: Rosie and I met over lunch soon after this column was published. Not much was settled at that time, in terms of our differences. But it opened up a dialogue, and I learned a lot. As another column in this collection explains, Rosie, like many people who come out publicly, went on her own positive journey over time.

WHAT GAY MEDIA?

WHEN A NATIONWIDE MANHUNT ensued for a spree killer shortly after the designer Gianni Versace was killed in 1997—during the height of the Clinton era, a time in which we were heralding the gay-rights movement's supposedly having arrived—Tom Brokaw, on *NBC Nightly News,* warned millions of people to be on the lookout for a "homicidal homosexual." Brokaw was talking about the suspect, Andrew Cunanan, who was gay, and he conjured up every dark Hollywood fabrication about murderous sexual deviants.

Could you imagine Brokaw saying "a homicidal Jew" was on the loose? Not likely in 1997, but it certainly was how, seventy or so years ago, the media in Europe and America would have described a murderer who happened to be Jewish. Brokaw's words underscore how far the media have to go in dealing with gays and lesbians, *Will & Grace* and civil-union announcements notwithstanding.

The media's treatment of gay issues popped into my head recently as I read Eric Alterman's *What Liberal Media?: The Truth About Bias and the News.* I wrote a column last week about *What Liberal Media?,* noting that the insightful and gutsy book skillfully destroys the liberal-media myth. On the issue of media bias and gay rights, however, Alterman is off base. It's not a major flaw in the book, but it needs to be addressed.

Conceding that the right may be correct in at least some of its charges, Alterman claims that the "overall flavor of the elite media reporting favors . . . gay rights" in addition to other issues, such as "gun control" and the "environmental move-ment." Though he doesn't "find this bias as overwhelming as some conservative critics do," he still believes it exists.

Just because reporters, editors, and TV news producers in the media are finally covering the gay-civil-rights movement—after decades of blackout—doesn't necessarily mean they favor gay rights. And coverage of gay issues seems to have dropped off in the past few years. Gays were the "flavor," alright—the flavor of the month.

Moreover, even if reporters and editors are more likely to be in favor of equal rights for gays, it doesn't mean that they are comfortable with homosexuality. Alterman is careful not to include race among those few issues about which he concedes the media have a liberal bias, perhaps understanding that even if reporters might be supportive of civil rights for African-Americans, it doesn't mean they deal very well with the highly charged issue of race.

"The nitty-gritty problem of how to handle race in the

media remains one that can make even the smartest people look stupid," he rightly notes.

I'd argue it's exactly the same with regard to the gay issue. Unlike "gun control," race, sexual orientation, and gender are issues about which most people harbor conditioned, emotion-based biases even after they have intellectually embraced ideas that challenge those biases. And in times when quick decisions are necessary, it is those embedded biases that often have editors and reporters reverting back to base stereotypes, even if unconsciously. The case of Tom Brokaw and Andrew Cunanan is a stellar example. And it's par for the course.

Usually, it's around issues of physical intimacy that the media break down entirely in covering gays, as if sexual anxiety suddenly takes over and rational thought goes out the window. When Ellen DeGeneres and Anne Heche nuzzled one another in front of Bill Clinton in 1997, the *New York Times*—that bastion of the so-called liberal media—wasted precious space on its editorial page to criticize the duo for supposedly inappropriate behavior, as if we've not seen heterosexuals nuzzling and doing a lot more in public ad nauseam. (Just think Al and Tipper Gore.)

More recently, sexual meltdowns ensued among sportswriters when two blind items buried in a silly tabloid implied that Mike Piazza and Sandy Koufax are gay, resulting in heated overreactions, forced denials, and lots of sanctimony when a simple clarification—or no response at all—was appropriate. And much of the media last year allowed the Catholic Church to blame its pedophile scandal on gay priests without strongly challenging this scapegoating.

In *What Liberal Media?,* as in past articles and blog entries, Alterman is quick to attack Andrew Sullivan for a 1999 *Times* opinion piece in which Sullivan questioned public figures who refused to acknowledge their sexual orientation at that time, like Rosie O'Donnell. Sullivan is a nasty, dishonest pundit—and Alterman is on target about everything else he's attacked Sullivan on—but that *Times* piece was actually one of the few critiques Sullivan made with which I and a great many gay leftists, liberals, and moderates agreed. He offered a criticism of the closet as an institution, discussed how society keeps it in place, and challenged some prominent individuals to come out. (Ten years ago, it should be noted, he attacked many of us on the gay left for making the same arguments, but he has never acknowledged his change of heart.)

For Alterman, it is, understandably, all political, with Sullivan using the *Times* to "out as gay two Clinton Cabinet members and liberal Democrats like Rosie O'Donnell." But hey, I was hard on Rosie, too, and I'm a dyed-in-the-wool Democrat. And some of the people Sullivan discussed, like former New York mayor Ed Koch, had been hostile toward the gay and AIDS movements and were outed years earlier, by that gay firebrand Larry Kramer. The gay movement in the 1990s redefined notions of privacy that had been ensconced in the larger left for decades. Even if you disagree with those new ideas, they should be acknowledged.

The left's press—the true liberal media—has had a checkered past on gay issues (though, of course, not as bad as the right's). The *Nation*'s coverage of AIDS as a political crisis was abysmal in the early years of the epidemic, as was the *Village Voice*'s, as noted in former CNN reporter Edward Alwood's seminal 1995 book *Straight News: Gays, Lesbians, and the News Media.* There are a lot of reasons for that, too numerous to go into now, and both publications have changed dramatically for the better over the years.

But one of the newest incarnations of the left's media—*Salon*—has showcased gay columnists such as Camille Paglia,

Norah Vincent, and Andrew Sullivan, all of whom are vociferously hostile toward the gay-rights movement and have championed conservative causes. The online publication has also run columnists such as David Horowitz, who has attacked gays and AIDS activists in bitter, offensive tirades. It's akin to having three Clarence Thomases and a David Duke writing on racial issues, without having any well-known black liberal columnist —and this is supposed to be the actual liberal media!

So, Alterman got that one wrong. But *What Liberal Media?* is a triumph nonetheless.

New York Press, **March 15, 2003**

WARTIME EXPOSES MILITARY HYPOCRISY ON GAYS

MORE THAN AT ANY other time, unit cohesion among the troops is paramount during war. For that reason, you would think that the armed services would be clamping down even harder on open homosexuality—which the Pentagon claims disrupts unit cohesion—and booting out record numbers of gay and lesbian service people.

But the opposite seems to be happening: Gay witch-hunts are down. Rather than speedily drumming out gays based on rumors or overheard declarations—the essence of the "don't ask, don't tell" policy—the military in some cases even appears intent on proving that service people aren't gay, even after the individuals claim to be.

With the war on, the military apparently needs every good man and woman it can get, no matter their sexual orientation —underscoring the hypocrisy of the "don't ask, don't tell" policy. Times have changed, and to many heterosexuals in the military, open gays are fine as long as they do their jobs as well as everyone else.

Take U.S. Army Sergeant Scott Osborn, a sixteen-year military veteran who spent the past ten years in the National Guard and the Reserves. He told his commander in December that he is gay. Under "don't ask, don't tell," he should have been kicked out pronto.

But, with war looming, the Army not only didn't immediately begin discharge proceedings; Osborn says it launched an investigation to see if he was indeed telling the truth or just trying to avoid being sent into combat. In the meantime, he was called to active duty and sent to Fort Bragg, North Carolina. The investigation eventually confirmed he was indeed gay, he says, and his commander, following orders, recommended that he be "separated."

Even so, Osborn says he was about to be shipped out to Kuwait. It wasn't until he gave an interview to the New York weekly *Gay City News*—discussing how he had been openly gay at Fort Bragg, was accepted as such by his higher-ups, and was about to be deployed—that he was discharged quickly. Osborn says he knows other gay and lesbian service people who are serving openly, some fighting in Iraq.

That claim is perhaps backed up by a new report from the Servicemembers Legal Defense Network (SLDN), which notes that the Pentagon's gay witch-hunts dramatically declined last year, as the war drums were beating. In 2001, 1,273 people were investigated and discharged for homosexuality. Last year, only 906 were booted out.

"During any time of war or conflict, gay discharges have dropped," the report observes. "Gay discharges decreased during the Korean War, the Viet Nam conflict, the Persian Gulf War, and now again during Operation Enduring Freedom."

It's true that there have been some high-profile cases in recent months in which the Pentagon hastily kicked out skilled people who could be important to the war effort, such as the Arabic linguists who received a lot of press coverage last summer.

But the overall trend seems to be to quietly use highly trained gay service people in times of need, only to discharge them when it's more convenient. During the first Persian Gulf War, the armed services issued a stop-loss order, which meant that most kinds of discharges, including for homosexuality, were put on hold for the duration of the war. Gay and lesbian soldiers served openly, only to be booted out when they returned home as heroes.

Under criticism from both gay activists and social conservatives, the various branches of the service this time around issued stop-loss orders that exclude gays, theoretically allowing for gay discharges to continue. Still, the SLDN report—and stories such as Osborn's—may indicate that there is an unofficial flouting of "don't ask, don't tell." Like Osborn, Army linguist Cathleen Glover came out to her commander last September, remained in the military, and continued working. It wasn't until November, after she wrote an op-ed piece for a California newspaper, that the military began its discharge proceedings.

The Pentagon has long claimed that heterosexuals in the military will experience so much sexual anxiety if gays are allowed to be open that it will adversely affect the military's work—the "unit cohesion" argument. That has been countered by calls to educate and sensitize service people on the issue of sexual orientation, as is done on the issues of race and gender.

But the contention itself may be overblown, since unit cohesion would be more crucial in a time of war than at any other time. Yet, wartime is precisely when the Pentagon gets lax on discharges. If open gays and lesbians are good enough to serve in wartime, they should be good enough to serve at any time.

Newsday, **April 2, 2003**

ROSIE RISING

WOULD THE MEDIA GIANT Gruner + Jahr have decided to sue Rosie O'Donnell over the downfall of *Rosie* magazine if same-sex marriage were legal? Bizarre as it might sound, Rosie believes the answer is no, and her explanation is both fascinating and plausible.

"If you are a heterosexual talk-show host and you're sued by a major corporation, anything you have said to your husband is privileged information," she said in an interview on my radio program on Sirius OutQ last week. She was referring to two rights of marriage that few of us ever think about—until we're sued for $100 million, or brought to court for something far more minor. One is the spousal immunity privilege, which, if you watch enough *Law & Order* or *The Practice,* you know means that, in general, a husband cannot be compelled to testify against his wife and vice versa. The other is known as "the privilege for marital communications," which protects confidential correspondence between spouses. These are just two of hundreds of rights granted by marriage—rights that gay couples don't have.

"If you are a homosexual talk-show host," O'Donnell continued, "and you're sued by a corporation, anything you have ever said and/or written to your spouse/partner/wife is allowed to be entered into the record. It is totally unfair."

She believes that Gruner + Jahr's lawyers were well aware of that inequity and exploited it to their advantage:

> Any and every thing I wrote to [my partner] Kelli, you know, which they were using against me, some of my essays—you know, when you get into a deep, dark place and you say, "You know what honey, blah, blah, blah, blah, blah." Well, if the honey is the same sex as you, that is evidence in a trial, and that's hard to believe in America. . . . And if they didn't have access to some of those letters I wrote to Kelli, I don't think they would have sued me. Because, innately, what they were thinking was that I would rather give them money than show the truth of my darkest part to America. . . ."

But if that were the case, the company was wrong in its assessment, as O'Donnell didn't back down and called their bluff. A judge indicated last month that he didn't think damages were in order.

The affair turned her into a promoter of same-sex marriage, though she'd previously been on the fence. "Never in my wildest dreams, if you said to me you're going to become an advocate for gay marriage, I'd say you're on crack," she told me. "But frankly, you need to be legally protected as a family, and my family was not legally protected."

Now Rosie's gone from the "queen of nice" who never talked about her sapphic desires, to a crusader for gay adoption, a promoter of same-sex marriage, and the producer of *Taboo,* the queerest play to hit Broadway in years. Along the way, she's been brutally attacked (almost as harshly as *Taboo* has been ripped apart by the critics) and ridiculed for shedding her former sweetness for the role of loudmouth dyke. Some of the nastiest barbs, particularly about her "bitch" demeanor, have come from gay male writers and theater critics (some of them circumspect about their own sexuality), thereby furthering the worst stereotypes about gay men as mincing misogynists.

I say this as someone who was one of Rosie's vocal detractors in the days when she was pining about Tom Cruise on her talk show. I have also been cynical on several occasions in this column about her media-managed coming out last year, which seemed designed to garner maximum exposure for her book. More than that, she appeared to deny the fact that she'd ever been closeted, and generally sloughed off the importance of coming out.

Those were pretty good grounds for criticism. But now that she's gone public, has admitted in the *Advocate* that she should have come out sooner, and become outspoken on gay political issues—not to mention her regular skewering of George W. Bush—why are some gay men attacking her even more fiercely than before? Are they embarrassed by her abrasiveness?

It's funny, but as she's coarsened in the mainstream, Rosie's become far more tender toward gay people. When I criticized her last year following her high-profile coming out, she called me a "moron." We eventually exchanged heated e-mails, and soon even met for lunch—takeout spinach salads in her office—during the last few weeks of her talk show. It was one of those impassioned conversations between two New Yorkers with big traps, and it didn't settle anything. But over the next few months Rosie went through a transformation, one that a lot of people go through when they finally bust out of the closet.

"Kelli and I went to P-town [Provincetown, Massachusetts] for the first time after the show ended," she said last week. "And I was amazed at the place . . . I got this feeling of community from the gay community that I hadn't really felt ever, because I really didn't get to do what normal people do when they come out. . . . I do think that my pleasure in being involved in the gay community now is . . . huge."

She's since given a hundred grand to the National Gay and Lesbian Task Force, visited the kids at the Harvey Milk High School for Gay Youth, and donated $25,000 to the school. She emceed the Hetrick-Martin Institute's Emery Awards a couple of weeks ago and she continues to advocate on the issue of gay adoption. Now she's taking up the cause of same-sex marriage at a time when the right wing is pushing a federal marriage amendment and the Democrats are running scared.

Hell, she's even saying some nicer things about us morons.

"You've been a very interesting guy to get to know and I want to thank you very much," she said on my show. "Just remember this: A lot of gay boys don't play on sports teams, so they don't know that when somebody's sitting on the bench, in uniform, they're still on your team, even though they're not scoring the points. So don't hurt them."

Okay, I get the point. I'm just glad she's off the bench now, and stepping up to the plate.

New York Press, **December 16, 2003**

OUTING HITLER

IN THE FALL OF 2001, the terrorist attacks led to the cancellation of a slew of book tours. But one book that broke through the blanket coverage and even snagged a *Today Show* interview within a few weeks of Sept. 11 was German historian Lothar Machtan's *The Hidden Hitler*. For a sensation-stalking media, even a monumental terrorist attack couldn't suppress the highly controversial premise of the book: that Adolf Hitler may have been a closeted homosexual.

It also proved irresistible stuff for late-night comedy, particularly at a time when everyone needed a good snicker. *Saturday Night Live* soon featured Chris Kattan in a pink SS uniform, prancing around the Third Reich, humping someone's leg.

Cute, but many gay activists weren't laughing. In the next few weeks, they'll be laughing even less. On April 20, Cinemax airs *The Hidden Führer: Debating the Enigma of Hitler's Sexuality,* an extensive documentary that draws upon Machtan's work and adds more grist for the mill, including claims that Hitler molested composer Richard Wagner's 18-year-old grandson. The filmmakers, Fenton Bailey and Randy Barbato (*Party Monster* and *The Eyes of Tammy Faye*), and author and journalist Gabriel Rotello, are gay themselves and certainly aren't averse to exploring controversial topics. (Full disclosure: I appear briefly in the film. All three filmmakers are longtime colleagues of mine.)

To a lot of gay activists and scholars, this isn't just another case of a dubious Bad Gay being exhumed; this is the Bad Mother Lode. Even before *The Hidden Hitler* was published in 2001, the Gay and Lesbian Alliance Against Defamation launched a blistering attack on Machtan, who is not gay but who, most critics agree, is not homophobic.

"[Machtan's] speculation fuels an ongoing debate that the person who still personifies evil and hate six decades later was one of us," said GLAAD's media director Cathy Renna, adding that the book is "without any real proof." In the *Washington Post,* Geoffrey Giles, associate professor of history at the University of Florida, accused Machtan of gathering up "every piece of malicious tittle-tattle and idle gossip," even though Giles admitted, "we can never know" the real truth about Hitler's sexuality.

There's a rightful skepticism among gays when an evildoer, dead or alive, is outed in the popular press. That's because journalists are usually loath to report on public figures' undeclared sexual orientation, piously claiming to be respectful of privacy —except, all too often, when it's a Bad Gay. When a 1993 biography claimed that the dictatorial FBI director J. Edgar Hoover not only was gay, but had a penchant for secretly donning cocktail dresses and feather boas, there seemed to be a collective exclamation: "Aha! He was a drag queen!" As if that somehow explained it all. Similarly, on the *Today* show, Matt Lauer teased his interview with Machtan by saying that *The Hidden Hitler* "claims that Hitler was actually gay, and that his homosexuality was at the root of his evil." The book claims nothing of the kind.

The impulse among some straights to pathologize homosexuality creates a strong resistance among many gays and lesbians to even entertain a premise. I've been guilty of that myself, writing on the 9/11 hijacker Mohamed Atta. At about the same time that *The Hidden Hitler* was published, a rumor began circulating that law enforcement was studying the possibility that the hijacking ringleader and some of his terrorist comrades were homosexual—a rumor investigators have neither confirmed nor denied. Atta had been described in the media shortly after the attacks as a squishy mama's boy whose father felt he wasn't man enough to be a terrorist.

The gay rumors were recycled by the *National Enquirer,* which reported that the FBI believed that "Atta and several of his bloody henchmen led secret gay lives for years." I followed up with a piece for Newsweek.com, noting that the rumors looked like more stereotyping on the part of federal law enforcement, which has a history of equating homosexuality with criminal activity going back to Hoover's days, and concluding that it shouldn't matter if Atta and his fellow hijackers were gay or not. But I was taking the point too far—just as the defensive critics of *The Hidden Hitler* are taking their point too far.

Of course it would matter if Atta were a homosexual. It would shed a bright light on how homophobia—not homosexuality—

may be a contributing factor in driving an individual to unfathomable destruction. If Atta and his homicidal companions were secretly homosexual, living within an Islamic fundamentalist society that often imprisons or beheads suspected sodomites, it might help explain why they gravitated toward organizations that adhered to the strictest and most extreme tenets of Islam, perhaps as a way to control their urges. And it also might explain why they'd so easily give up their lives rather than continue in their tortured existences.

In the case of Hitler, such knowledge would be profoundly revelatory as well. In Machtan's portrait, Hitler was perhaps so self-loathing and so traumatized by the fear of exposure that he'd do anything to prove he wasn't a homosexual, including, later, persecuting other gays and violently stopping anyone, straight or gay, who might expose him as he rose to power. Machtan even posits that the SA chief Ernst Röhm, who was openly homosexual, was killed in the infamous Night of the Long Knives on Hitler's orders because Hitler was afraid Röhm was going to out him. It may sound far-fetched, but that formula—squashing other gays as you grab for the brass ring—is a tried-and-true one among the closeted and power-hungry set. It's the same formula used by Roy Cohn, Senator Joseph McCarthy's sidekick, in his purges of gays in government as he ascended to the power elite.

The Cinemax documentary powerfully distills the evidence in a way that Machtan's book doesn't. *The Hidden Führer* doesn't prove that Hitler was gay, but it certainly gives you a lot to chew on. One flaw, however, is that it doesn't explore why this is important to know. Midway through *The Hidden Führer,* you're convinced that there's something there, but you're left wondering what the point is and why so many gays don't want to know.

In the cases of other, more laudable public figures—from

Leonardo da Vinci and Walt Whitman to Florence Nightingale and Susan B. Anthony—gay activists and gay historians haven't had a problem claiming them as lesbian or gay. The proof hasn't always been definitive for the straight world, even if it has been for many gay activists and gay academics. Because Eleanor Roosevelt was close with several lesbian couples and wrote highly affectionate letters to a constant companion, Lorena Hickok, the First Lady was, according to many gay history books and Web sites, a lesbian—though some might say the evidence of that isn't any stronger than that presented regarding Hitler.

That's why the critics' angry denunciations ring a bit hollow. And with books like Machtan's and films like *The Hidden Führer* making the case, dismissing it isn't going to make the question go away. Why not engage the debate and see where it leads?

New York Press, **April 12, 2004**

THE SICK-PUPPY DEFENSE

CONSERVATIVE MEDIA PUNDITS REVEL in their "personal responsibility" and "stand up like a man" mantras. But when the spotlight shines on one of their own, they quickly become the epitome of the lame stereotypes they have long perpetrated of the whining, sissy-boy left, blaming everyone but themselves for the problems that ail us.

Case in point: After days of silence on the abuse by American soldiers of Iraqi prisoners and the detrimental affect it will have on U.S. national security, the conservative *National Review* ran a piece online by Jonah Goldberg, trying to offer us some "context" for these crimes.

In Goldberg Land, who do you suppose is to blame for the

abuse and the ensuing public-relations disaster? Was it the president, for taking us to war based on false claims about weapons of mass destruction, incurring the wrath of Muslims in the region and thus opening us up to even more hatred and violence should something like this abuse occur? Was it Donald Rumsfeld, for doing the war on the cheap, allowing the command to break down, leaving many tasks to civilian private contractors who could operate without any authority and covering up reports of wrongdoing from Congress?

No, the true culprit was CBS.

"Of course, CBS had every right to do what it did," Goldberg wrote, discussing the airing of the photographs of the brutality. "But that's irrelevant. Nobody's suggesting the government should have stopped them. I'm suggesting that CBS should have stopped itself. Now we'll all have to live with the consequences—and some of us will die from them."

In Goldberg Land, "when shocking images might stir Americans to favor war"—such as those depicting people jumping from the Twin Towers during the 9/11 attacks and those showing the charred bodies of American civilian contractors in Iraq—"the Serious Journalists show great restraint." But, Goldberg claims, "when those shocking images have the opposite effect, the Ted Koppels let it fly."

I don't know about you, but I recall seeing the images of the people jumping from the windows of the Twin Towers—on television and certainly in newspapers—over and over again, until the families of the victims finally complained to the media about insensitivity and sheer overkill. No one asked for the footage to be censored as a way of inhibiting war, which, in the case of Afghanistan, the vast majority of Americans (including just about every liberal-media pundit) were in favor of, and still are to this day. As far as the destruction of the buildings goes, we've seen that from every angle and still do, in news programs and documentaries. And it was on the front page of the *New York Times*—the paper that right-wing conservatives view as the Bush-hating, antiwar organ—where I saw the photos of the burned bodies of the contractors a few weeks ago.

But put a hole in one of the conservatives' offensive theories about who's to blame for the brutality of the Iraqi prisoners, and they'll spin out yet another one. If it's not CBS and the rest of the "liberal media" that is at fault, then surely it must be Bill Clinton and the homosexuals, right? Last week, I actually heard right-wing radio chat while in a taxi, in which callers and the host agreed that we wouldn't have seen this kind of "homosexual" brutality against the prisoners "if Bill Clinton had not let homosexuals into the military." And if the torturers are not gay themselves, then surely they're a product of the "Clinton era" and its homo-loving policies, says James Taranto, the often-idiotic moralizer at the *Wall Street Journal*'s OpinionJournal. A link to Taranto's attempts to blame the barbaric soldiers' actions on the American academic left had me cackling with laughter soon after it came to me in my e-mail box. Get this:

> [I]t also occurs to us that increasing the quality of military recruits would probably help avoid future Abu Ghraibs. One constructive step toward that end would be for elite universities to drop antimilitary policies, so that the military would have an easier time signing up the best and brightest young Americans. Many academic institutions have barred ROTC or military recruiters from campus for left-wing political reasons—first as a protest against the Vietnam War, and later over the Clinton-era "don't ask, don't tell" law. Whatever the merits of these

positions, it's time the academic left showed some patriotic responsibility and acknowledged that the defense of the country—which includes the defense of their own academic freedom—is more important than the issue du jour.

Could anybody make more of a stretch in attempting to demonize those he despises while deflecting criticism of his own? Well, there's always Ann Coulter. Via David Brock's terrific new MediaMatters.org Web site—which is focused on all of the bile spewers on the right—I found this quote from Coulter, speaking on Fox News and blaming the soldiers' brutality on women: "I think the other point that no one is making about the abuse photos is just the disproportionate number of women involved, including a girl general running the entire operation. I mean, this is a lesson, you know, 1,000,047 on why women shouldn't be in the military. In addition to not being able to carry even a medium-sized backpack, women are too vicious."

Similarly, the antifeminist columnist Linda Chavez—George W. Bush's onetime Labor Secretary nominee, who withdrew when she was found to be paying an illegal immigrant housekeeper off the books—suggested that "the presence of women in the unit actually encouraged more misbehavior, especially of the sexual nature that the pictures reveal."

Another conservative finger-pointer seemed to get Rush Limbaugh all hot and sweaty during his weeklong quest to downplay the images as nothing more than college frat-boy games. Donna M. Hughes, on *National Review* online, asked, "Why are we shocked by these images from Abu Ghraib, but when the victims are women (or gay men) the images are called pornography or 'adult entertainment'?" Yes, she was attempting to explain and excuse the behavior—and give anti-porn crusader John Ashcroft more grist for his twisted mill—by claiming that the reservists might have engaged in these acts of torture because they'd seen them played out in porn films. (Of course, according to that logic we should ban *The Passion of the Christ,* because if people played out the sadomasochistic scenes in that film, we'd be taking down bloody crosses from every street corner.)

That got Limbaugh thinking and making some lurid confessions:

> If you look at these pictures, you cannot deny that there are elements of homoeroticism. . . . I've seen things like this on American Web sites. You can find these if you have the passwords to these various porn sites, you can see things like this. And [Hughes's] point was maybe these kids—the soldiers, the guards, whoever, who are of a certain age group, who've grown up with access to this are simply acting out what they've seen on these Web sites or something, just for the fun of it, or maybe other reasons.

Another crackpot deflection regarding the brutality, to be sure. But now we also know what Limbaugh was doing on those OxyContin-dazed nights: fumbling for his passwords, looking for those homoerotic Web sites. Live and learn.

New York Press, **May 11, 2004**

THAT HELL-BOUND TRAIN

WHAT A DIFFERENCE A year—and the truth—makes, huh? A measly 365 days ago, if you believed there were no weapons of mass destruction in Iraq, you were a nut-job, a dangerous leftist ideologue and/or on Osama bin Laden's or Saddam Hussein's payroll. Perhaps you were one of Andrew Sullivan's "fifth column" of pundits trying to undermine the president. Or maybe you were one of those traitors who should have been bombed yourself, as Ann Coulter opined back in August of 2002 regarding the supposedly liberal editors and reporters at the *New York Times*. Much of the rabid right, including the *Wall Street Journal* editorial page, looked on, snickering and defending Annie on that one. They probably agreed with her when she accused liberals of treason for questioning the war and the weapons claims.

But now, here we have none other than George W. Bush's own weapons monitor in Iraq, David Kay, stepping down and confirming what experts from former U.N. chief inspector Hans Blix (accused of conspiring with the dreaded French) to Scott Ritter (the former U.N. weapons inspector whom conservatives portrayed as a kook via an all-too-willing media) had said: Iraq had no weapons of mass destruction prior to the war and that the Bushies were "almost all wrong."

It was only last year when Kay was goring Blix and insinuating there were plenty of WMDs to find. But clearly Kay decided he had to save whatever was left of his reputation after falling in with the wrong crowd—he even admitted that some of his staff were "almost in tears," saying they felt so bad over not finding weapons—so he hit the talk-show circuit and congressional committees. As a rightly smug Blix cracked about Kay's turnaround last week: "I was beginning to wonder what was going on. Weren't they wondering, too? If you find yourself on a train that's going in the wrong direction, it's best to get off at the next stop."

The White House, however, is continuing full speed ahead on the runaway train, with Donald Rumsfeld and Dick Cheney as the conductors, and Colin Powell having sold the one-way tickets for the trip straight into a hellish quagmire. (Think of Bush as a sort of eccentric passenger going along for the ride, sitting up in first class, actually imagining he's the president of the United States.)

Kay gave the Bushies some cover, claiming it was all an intelligence problem and that he doesn't think Bush and company manipulated the CIA into delivering what the war hawks wanted. The right-wing pundits have gone into defense mode, attacking anyone who points to the administration's cooking the intelligence and slamming anyone accusing Bush of lying. They're all counting on media laziness—which has certainly helped in the past—but all you have to do is go back to the many reports leading up to the war to see that what we're witnessing now is just more of the grand farce.

"Interviews with administration officials revealed divisions between, on one side, the Pentagon and the National Security Council, which has become a clearinghouse for the evidence being prepared for Mr. Powell, and, on the other, the C.I.A. and, to some degree, the State Department and agencies like the F.B.I.," the *Times* reported on February 2 of last year. That was right before Powell gave his now-bogus speech about "mobile production systems mounted on road trailer units" that "can produce enough dry biological agent in a single month to kill thousands upon thousands of people"—the trailers of mass destruction that Kay now confirms were used for making weather balloons.

The *Times* reported:

> In the interviews, two officials, Paul D. Wolfowitz, deputy defense secretary, and Stephen J. Hadley, deputy national security adviser, were cited as being most eager to interpret evidence deemed murky by intelligence officials to show a clearer picture of Iraq's involvement in illicit weapons programs and terrorism. Their bosses, Defense Secretary Donald H. Rumsfeld and the national security adviser, Condoleezza Rice, have also pressed a hard line, officials said. . . . "It's more than just skepticism," said one official, describing the feelings of some analysts in the intelligence agencies. "I think there is also a

sense of disappointment with the community's leadership that they are not standing up for them at a
time when the intelligence is obviously being
politicized.' "

That's just one of dozens of reports throughout a variety of
media at the time, all of which pointed to the fact that the Bush
administration was marching to war using whatever it could
scrape out of the CIA. The hawks were planning the invasion
of Iraq within weeks of Bush's inauguration, according to
former treasury secretary Paul O'Neill, and were looking for
the intelligence to back them up. Let's not forget, too, that
within hours of the 9/11 attacks, Rumsfeld was trying to blame
Saddam and launch an attack on Iraq. The fact that all of this is
even up for debate now is really quite laughable.

In addition to the "faulty intelligence" ruse, conservatives are
also defending Bush by pulling out their old standby argument:
"But Bill Clinton . . ." (Actually, blaming the CIA is blaming
Clinton as well, since CIA director George Tenet is a Clinton
holdover, and a lot of Republicans in Congress want to get rid
of him.) The supposedly faulty intelligence on WMDs in Iraq
was the same intelligence used under the Clinton administration, they're claiming, and foreign governments believed it, too.
But if you follow the time line in Kay's remarks, Saddam likely
did have stockpiles of WMDs during the early part of the
Clinton presidency. Sanctions, U.N. inspections, internal cor-
ruption, and Saddam's overall lunacy, however, contributed to
Iraq's dismantling, and/or not proceeding with, nuclear programs by decade's end. Another thing happened as well: In the
mid-1990s, according to Kay, a targeted bombing campaign by
the United States destroyed most or all of Saddam's chemical
weapons.

"The large chemical overhang of existing stockpiles was eliminated," Kay said.

In other words, Bill Clinton, scourge of the right and one of those soft-on-terrorism Democrats, actually can take credit for ending Saddam's illicit weapons programs. Even if Clinton, France, Germany, and others believed right up until the war last year that Saddam still had WMDs, those beliefs were based on intelligence that, rightly, wasn't solid enough for any of them to support an invasion before more inspections could take place. As Kay told Ted Koppel on *Nightline*, if you're going to have a policy of "preemption" then the intelligence has to be "pristine." With CIA insiders complaining about intelligence being "politicized," and with Dick Cheney's hands constantly molding it—he was, according to reports last year, shuttling back and forth between the White House and the CIA—the intelligence was anything but.

Now Bush, who originally dismissed demands for an independent investigation, has announced a commission to look at broader intelligence problems, described by a White House official as focusing on "the global security challenges of the 21st century." That's perfectly tailored to divert attention and keep the focus off the White House and its misleading claims about Iraq. And it's so grand that it conveniently can't be completed by November, allowing Bush to continue to deflect criticism through the election. The White House knows that if we go back now and retrace all the steps, the lies and the shams will materialize faster than any weapons of mass destruction have.

New York Press, **February 3, 2004**

DEAR MARY: AN OPEN LETTER TO THE VICE PRESIDENT'S DAUGHTER

EXCUSE ME FOR BEING blunt, but my rights are at stake at the moment, as our born-again president has told his theocratic mentors that he'd sell us—you, me, and millions of other homos—down the river. So let's get to the point: What the hell happened to you? Are you just another spoiled rich brat—the lesbian Paris Hilton—worried about getting a chunk of those 30 million Halliburton bucks should Dad's heart conk out? I mean, this is one of those moments of truth, Mary, one in which the fundamentalist forces of darkness either march into the White House—enshrining antigay discrimination into the U.S. Constitution—or are beaten back. And so far, you've been working for the enemy, darling.

You may be banking on the idea that people will cut you some slack.

"None of us can imagine how hard it would be to find ourselves between our family and our community," one of your friends—a mutual friend of ours, actually—told the *Advocate* last year. "It would cause anyone tremendous heartache."

You may think that kind of sympathy will carry through this election season. Don't count on it.

Quite frankly, you owe us, Mary. Big time. And you better believe that people—including many a gay Republican, at least if my e-mail inbox is any indication—will be coming to get you, demanding that you fork over that debt, pronto. Unless you speak out now, every time your father or the president or Karl Rove stokes antigay hatred in the coming campaign, folks will be pointing fingers at you and asking, "What the fuck, Mary?!" Perhaps you don't have a conscience and none of this will affect you. But the next time you walk into a gay public place, be prepared for a chorus calling you everything from a quisling and a betrayer to a selfish, fiendish, nasty example of a human being.

It would be one thing if you had simply slithered away into the background when it was announced that your father would be Bush's running mate in 2000. (People can't, after all, pick their parents, as Patti Davis and Ron Reagan, Jr. are painfully aware.) Instead, you became active in the Bush/Cheney campaign. As the lesbian poster child, you helped sell the snake oil of "compassionate conservatism." You went along with the program, tricking people into thinking that your father and W. would be tolerant on gay rights. Your father even said during the campaign that the whole issue of gay unions should be left to the states (though he told the *Denver Post* last week that he would now support an amendment to the Constitution that could very well strip gays of most legal rights, from domestic-partnership benefits to adoption rights). As one of Dad's political advisers, you helped bring in votes from moderate straights and gay Republicans.

Yes, Mary, I'm laying part of the blame for the 2000 election fiasco on you. Had the election not been so close, it wouldn't have been so easy to steal. And it was close, in part, because you conned a lot of people. The 25 percent of gay voters who cast a vote for Bush/Cheney—not to mention the moderates of all sexual orientations—would have made the difference in Florida and New Hampshire (as gays made up at least 4 percent of the electorate in both states), giving the election to Al Gore. I hear from the voters you misled every day via my Web site and radio program—gay Republicans and others who are infuriated with the president, with your father, and with you, Mary.

Some people—mostly Democrats, actually, who sometimes are just a bit too generous, if you ask me—have mildly defended you, claiming that you truly, if naïvely, believed you could make a difference. Shortly after the election, you joined the board of the Republican Unity Coalition, the gay/straight alliance. But at about the same time that the Christian zealots began complaining that Bush wasn't harsh enough toward gays, you left RUC and went as far underground as your father, who runs things from his mystery bunker as often as from the White House.

And now you've joined the reelection campaign, just in time to hear the president and your father say that they would support a federal marriage amendment.

What is it like, I often wonder, to have your own father court the very religious zealots who believe your kind are emotionally disturbed child molesters? What does it feel like to have your own father empower people who, if they could have their way, would force you to go through "conversion therapy"?

What is it like to know that your own family takes cash from people who think you'd be better off dead, and think you're going straight to hell when that happens?

Those who defend you say that you must feel absolutely terrible. They surmise that maybe you actually left RUC in protest, realizing that change in the party wasn't possible, thus washing your hands of the entire matter. For that reason, they say, you shouldn't now be blamed for trying, nor held accountable for your father's positions. But the fact that you went to work for the reelection campaign says otherwise.

So here's my theory, and maybe you can confirm it for me: The gay-marriage issue is splitting the Republican Party; Dad and his crowd have told you that they've got to appear to be supportive of a constitutional amendment at this point, while they're still firing up the religious-right base. Once they have that constituency nailed down and they enter the general election, they'll move toward the middle; they'll say that there's no need for the amendment, as the Defense of Marriage Act takes care of it. You'll then be hauled back out of the closet to help snatch those moderate and gay Republican voters.

Let's put aside the fact that Dad and company have lied before. Even if this scenario proves true, in the process there will be a lot of political gay-bashing, the kind that fuels the Christian right as well as thugs on the streets. The impact of that can't be underestimated, and yes, Mary, blood will be on your hands, too. I'm sure you think that's unfair of me. But life is unfair. Just think: You could be a poor dyke getting your head bashed in a rough, urban neighborhood every day of your life. Instead, you're a woman of privilege who has done a lot of damage and now needs to take responsibility for it by stepping down from the campaign and speaking up. History,

Mary, will judge you by what you choose to do in the coming
months.

New York Press, **February 3, 2004**

*Note: This column received a tremendous outpouring of support in the form of
thousands of e-mail messages from around the United States and from around
the world. It inspired a Web site, DearMary.com, founded by the Web activist
John Aravosis, designed for people to write their own letters to Mary Cheney.
The Web site received much media attention during the election campaign,
surely to the dismay of the Bush/Cheney campaign and Mary Cheney herself. I did send the column directly to Mary Cheney before it was published,
to two separate e-mail accounts that one of her associates had given me.*

She never responded.

THE *WASHINGTON* (END OF) *TIMES*

CAN YOU IMAGINE THE owners of the *New York Times*—or the *Los Angeles Times* or Cleveland's *Plain-Dealer*—pining out loud for the mass extinction of an entire group of people? Let's say they envisioned the incineration of all gays, claiming it was God's plan and had their words posted on the Web.

At the very least, sensation-stalker Matt Drudge would link to the comments immediately, rightly whipping it into a major story. His zeal for fomenting scandals involving liberals would certainly overpower his obsessive fear that people might think he's gay just for defending gays. (As if the rest of the world still doesn't know he's gay, even after David Brock's "fuck buddies" revelations and Jeannette Walls's interviews with his former boyfriends.) Drudge's openly gay compatriot, Andrew Sullivan, would no doubt take up the cause as well, attacking those nasty homophobe publishers on the left, railing on his Web site about what hypocrites liberals are.

But if the paper in question is an influential conservative daily—one that pumps up both of these right-wing gasbags regularly, and one that publishes Sullivan's work—then the rantings and ravings of its demagogic owner don't seem to matter.

"There will be a purge on God's orders, and evil will be eliminated like shadows," the Unification Church leader Reverend Sun Myung Moon, the owner and primary funder of the money-losing, right-wing *Washington Times,* said last week. (The comments were posted online by Reverend Moon's Webmaster and picked up by blogger John Gorenfeld.)

"Gays will be eliminated, the 3 Israels will unite. If not then they will be burned. We do not know what kind of world God will bring but this is what happens. It will be greater than the communist purge but at God's orders."

This isn't the first time this madman—who owns UPI as well—has thundered against gays and others. You may remember these ditties from the Moonie-in-chief, which I reported last year:

America is the kingdom of extreme individualism, the kingdom of free sex . . . The country that represents Satan's harvest is America.

[Homosexuals and] those who go after free sex [are] less than animals.

If you misuse your love organ, you destroy your life, your nation, your world.

If you stay away from having children, you cannot enter the kingdom of God. You are bound to go to somewhere else—you can call it Hell.

These diatribes haven't stopped Washington's conservatives from getting in bed with Moon—whose goal is to create a global theocracy, à la Muslim fundamentalists—and elevating his and his paper's stature in return for cold, hard cash for themselves and for their movement. George H. W. Bush took $100,000 from him in 1996 for a speaking engagement, praising the *Washington Times* as "a paper that in my view brings sanity to Washington, D.C." After Bush called Moon "the man with the vision," the reverend gave him $1 million for his presidential library.

Contrary to the claims of the paper's defenders on the right, a former editor reported recently that Moon has much more involvement in the paper than he and his apologists lead people to believe. Last June, Moon, who believes he's the "Messiah," launched a "special media training" for church leaders with the *Times*'s staff. The paper's editorial-page editor, former Newt Gingrich aide Tony Blankley—a man who tries to come off as a sane and reasoned, if staunchly conservative, individual, even though he works for a crackpot cultist—is all over the talk-show circuit, an example of how much influence the *Washington Times* has beyond its relatively small circulation. On C-Span last week, Blankley referred to the *Wall Street Journal* as having the nation's "other" influential conservative-newspaper editorial page, clearly noting how seriously his paper is taken in the corridors of power.

It's sleazy enough that a conservative would work for Moon and ignore his dark and dangerous agenda. But how on earth could a gay writer take a check from a man who can't wait to see him thrown into an oven? Andrew Sullivan has reveled in his own idiotic claim that after 9/11 certain liberals, because they didn't agree with George W. Bush's policies, represented a "fifth column" supporting Osama bin Laden. Meanwhile, here he is, on the payroll of a guy who would like to see the mass extinction of his own people. Sullivan likes to think of himself as a gay-rights activist—that's actually how *New York* magazine described him recently—but he seems to activate only when the targets are liberals. Bill Clinton gets the Sullivan hatchet treatment for signing the Defense of Marriage Act, while the grossly homophobic Unification Church's leader gets a weekly column from him in return for a few bucks to keep Sullivan's increasingly lackluster and predictable Web page afloat.

Equally duplicitous is the sexually circumspect Drudge, who draws credibility from the *Washington Times*'s numerous references and vice versa. He spent the better part of last week trying to frame liberals as belittling the Nazis and the Holocaust. For days he stoked a bogus story pushed by the Republican National Committee and the *Wall Street Journal* that claimed that the group MoveOn.org had created TV ads comparing Bush to Hitler. When the ads were gone from the group's Web site, the right-wingers claimed they had scored another victory, as when they got the cowardly CBS to ban *The Reagans.*

In fact, the ads were not sponsored by MoveOn.org, but were entries in a contest the group sponsored, "Bush in 30 Seconds," in which participants created ads illustrating the Bush administration's dismal failures. More than 1,500 entries came in, including two ads comparing Bush to Hitler, and all were available on the site for viewing. Neither of the overwrought, tasteless Hitler ads did well with the members who voted, and neither creators progressed as finalists in the contest. (Celebrity judges will choose a winner from the finalists.) And that's why they and the hundreds of others that didn't make the cut were no longer available on the site—not because of any sort of pressure campaign.

Drudge and company were nonetheless successful in spinning their lies into the mainstream press, with the lazy Judy Woodruff and others at CNN only too willing to report the RNC's talking points as objective news. Funny how Drudge blew up a fake story and expressed outrage about Bush being compared to a genocidal dictator, but then didn't find it newsworthy to link to the comments of a powerful newspaper owner, cult leader, and Bush family pal who is actually calling for genocide—of Drudge's own kind, no less.

Maybe Moon had told Drudge and Sullivan that they'll be spared on Judgment Day. Or maybe they just don't give a shit about anyone but themselves.

New York Press, **January 13, 2004**

AMERICA SHRUGGED

"BARRING A MIRACLE, THE family as it has been known for more than five millennia, will crumble," warned the evangelist and psychologist Dr. James Dobson, regarding Massachusetts's impending first state-sanctioned same-sex marriages. Promises, promises! May 17 came and went, and the last time I checked, the family was still standing, dysfunctional as ever. The world is still spinning on its axis, the American economy keeps sputtering along and Iraq continues to spiral out of control.

The End of Civilization has proven to be the biggest, most overhyped disappointment since the Y2K bug. No rapture, no floods, no earthquakes, no locusts. (Cicadas do not count.) The firstborn of every family did not die, nor did God strike

Massachusetts off the map with an almighty thunderbolt. The weather, from what I could gather, seemed unseasonably pleasant all the way to Provincetown, as thousands of gay and lesbian couples wed across the Bay State last week.

Evangelical leaders were hoping the pictures on television of gay couples getting hitched would sicken and outrage the masses, driving millions of Americans to the barricades to take on the enemy within.

"The attacks on Pearl Harbor, New York and Washington awakened the nation to peril and called citizens to action," said R. Albert Mohler Jr., president of the Southern Baptist Theological Seminary, comparing those attacks to the Massachusetts decision. (He even called May 17 "a day that will live in moral infamy.")

Judging from most people's reactions, it's a day that's already been forgotten. So the new tack by the goofy God Squad is to claim that people are in a state of shock, experiencing a delayed response.

"The fact is, enough people haven't awakened," the Reverend Lou Sheldon, founder of the Traditional Values Coalition, told the *Washington Post*. "It's a sleeping giant out there. . . . And when [people] wake up I feel bad for the homosexuals."

Actually, people *have* woken up, and they're quite revolted. But the same-gender photo pairings that got them sick to their stomachs weren't coming out of Massachusetts: They were the photos out of Abu Ghraib, depicting the humiliating simulated sex acts that American soldiers and civilian contractors—using homosexual sex in a grotesquely homophobic manner—forced male Iraqi detainees to engage in.

In that respect, the timing of the Massachusetts marriages couldn't have been better for the same-sex marriage movement. The prison-abuse scandal, the continuing violence in

Iraq, and the administration's handling of the war puts same-sex marriage in perspective for most people. George W. Bush's approval ratings have plummeted as Americans realize that it's not gay marriage that's destroying the country, but rather the president, Donald Rumsfeld, Condoleezza Rice, and the rest of the gang in the White House. *They're* the ones who've taken us to war based on lies and have irreparably damaged the nation's integrity.

In Congress, the Federal Marriage Amendment seems dead in the water. Perhaps it wasn't a coincidence that the Senate canceled a hearing on the amendment last week at which the homo-obsessed Governor Mitt Romney of Massachusetts was to appear. How would it look if, in the middle of all the turmoil in the Middle East, reports came out of Washington depicting our senators focused on an issue that ranks at the bottom of voters' lists of priorities in every poll?

Several months back, I wrote that the FMA could turn out to be more of a problem for Bush than John Kerry (who doesn't support same-sex marriage either), as most voters, no matter how they feel about gay unions, have little passion to amend the Constitution or even to waste much time debating the issue. That has turned out to be true, but I didn't foresee other factors that have further complicated the FMA from Bush's perspective. Several recent reports have noted that the proposed gay-marriage ban, while a major talking point for evangelical leaders, is failing to excite the evangelical rank and file. Even if they are adamantly opposed to same-sex marriage, many are ambivalent about getting the federal government involved. It's not a black-and-white issue for them, like abortion, nor is it one that gets them to empty their pockets and run to the polls.

"Just four months after an alliance of conservative Christians was threatening a churchgoer revolt unless President Bush championed an amendment banning same-sex marriage, members say they have been surprised and disappointed by what they call a tepid response from the pews," the *New York Times* reported.

If the FMA doesn't energize the GOP's religious base, and if the abortion issue doesn't fulfill that function either this year—Bush's chipping away at abortion rights might make some conservative Christians complacent in 2004—Bush may get the same turnout among evangelicals that he got in 2000, which was a disappointment to Karl Rove. Meanwhile, Bush will have alienated some moderate Republicans and Democrats who previously supported him. But perhaps more important, he will have energized many liberal Democrats and gay-rights advocates, who are organizing fiercely in light of his support of the FMA.

Gay groups on college campuses and in community centers across the country are briskly registering new voters, painting Bush as a tyrant who is turning gays into second-class citizens. The Human Rights Campaign, the largest gay group in Washington, last week launched an ad campaign excoriating Bush, which will appear more than eighty-five times in gay, lesbian, bisexual, and transgender community publications. Even the Log Cabin Republicans launched television commercials critical of Bush for supporting the amendment.

Most of those in the religious right who feel passionately about the FMA are voting for Bush anyway. It's quite possible that Bush's continued vocal support of the FMA will get more Democrats than Republicans out to vote—it's certainly energizing loyal Democratic constituencies like gays and lesbians. Meanwhile, the majority of voters, including swing voters, will only continue to note that Bush is trying to change the subject and focus on an issue that is not a priority for them. It's not that they support same-sex marriage necessarily—though the most recent *Newsweek* poll showed a slim majority supporting some form of legal sanction for gay unions—but seeing Bush pandering to the religious right while there are so many other issues affecting the country isn't going to play well. As an issue this election year, same-sex marriage may turn out to be a trap that Karl Rove set for Kerry, but which hapless W. walked into all by himself.

New York Press, **May 25, 2004**

HOMOSEXUAL GOVERNOR ON THE LOOSE!

I WAS AT HOME, taking a day off from my daily radio program, thinking it would be another slow news day in August. Silly me—there is a war on, after all, and we could have expected the California Supreme Court to nullify the 4,000 gay weddings out there any day now. So I was sitting in front of the computer, the television on my desk tuned in to CNN, when Jim McGreevey stepped to the podium. The big, bad closet is alive and well in America, and like Hurricane Charley on that same day, it was about to make itself felt.

Suddenly, my AOL overloaded with instant messages, the phone began ringing, the e-mails piling up. Ten minutes and what seemed like a hundred IMs later, CNN's Candi Crowley was talking about how McGreevey had just "admitted" to being homosexual, as if it were some sort of addiction or crime. Once again, the mainstream press was clueless. (It reminded me of when Tom Brokaw, reporting on Gianni Versace's killer Andrew Cunanan, warned America of a "homicidal homosexual" who was on the loose.) I headed up to the Sirius studios to break in to the rebroadcast of my show that we'd been airing, and I did the last hour of the show live.

The shocked and bewildered callers began the discussion, and the questions people were asking are the ones we're still asking days later. Who is the hero here? Who's the victim? Gay groups embraced McGreevey in his post–coming out, which seemed a bit weird, since he was not exactly a paragon of political virtue, and then seemed to use his homosexuality to his advantage.

Sure, he was now telling the truth and proudly calling himself "a gay American." But we then learned that he got the line from the Human Rights Campaign, the Washington-based gay group with which he'd apparently consulted in the days leading up to his speech, after they'd poll-tested the phrase. McGreevey was using his coming out to gain sympathy, and perhaps to deflect from other issues, still the opportunist he's always been. He'd hidden his homosexuality when it suited him, and he was now playing it up when it suited him as well.

But so what? Just about every politician is an opportunist—it's the bar we've set in American politics, after all—and there have been plenty of straight politicians who've given jobs to their girlfriends and certainly many more who've had extramarital sex that went public in a scandal. They didn't resign, and nor should McGreevey have resigned. It could have been the beginning of his career as a gay American governor—the first ever—unless, of course, he was just using this as an excuse to cut his losses and run, so embattled was he on so many other issues.

Then there's the alleged other man, Golan Cipel. McGreevey's aides have told the press that Cipel—the inexperienced Israeli citizen whom McGreevey had made his homeland-security adviser, touching off a firestorm of criticism—was trying to extort millions of dollars from him, claiming he'd file a lawsuit against McGreevey unless McGreevey paid up. Cipel's now saying he's straight, that the relationship was not consensual, and that he was sexually abused.

He seems like a two-bit hustler, but I can't help but also think of the many men I interviewed in 1990 for my first book, *Queer in America: Sex, the Media, and the Closets of Power*—men who worked for powerful closet cases in Washington. They were young, ambitious, and closeted themselves, and found themselves working as aides for elected officials who exploited their own confusion and self-hatred.

I remember, in particular, Keith, who worked for a male U.S. legislator who coerced him into sexual acts in return for advancement in his job. At the time, Keith still saw himself as straight, and couldn't understand the feelings he was having, nor why he continued in the job. But he certainly related at the time to Anita Hill, the woman who charged that Supreme Court Justice nominee Clarence Thomas sexually harassed her over a long period of time while she continued to work for him.

But I don't know about Cipel. He seems like too much of a smooth operator—living in a posh place on the Upper West Side, cavorting with and working for a known blackmailer (McGreevey fund-raiser Charles Kushner, who was charged with blackmailing his own brother-in-law), and, from what I'm told, being very out and about in all the gayest places in Chelsea. As new information comes out every day, McGreevey and Cipel both look sleazy—it seems like they indeed make the perfect couple.

It's sordid, but there is something to learn here. So many people, including gay people of younger generations who might be very open themselves, seem to think the closet is a relic of the past. But the truth is, the vast majority of gay Americans likely still live closeted existences just like Jim McGreevey did. A lot of the McGreevey media coverage has claimed that he's from "a different generation," a "throwback," etc., as if he grew up in the nineteenth century. In fact, McGreevey, who is forty-seven years old, grew up in the 1960s like the rest of the generation that is supposedly a product of the sexual revolution, the women's movement, and the gay-rights movement. He was fourteen in 1969, the year of Woodstock and the Stonewall riots.

We were to believe that there was a vast difference between the people of McGreevey's generation and those only ten years his senior, with their Eisenhower-era childhoods. What McGreevey shows us is that plenty of ambitious people, operating within a world that is still greatly homophobic and has not yet elected an openly gay governor to any state, are willing to lie and deceive themselves, often engaging in irrational behavior.

In fact, it may even be easier today to be closeted than it was in the past. As I wrote in this column a few months ago, the internet, for example, has provided a new forum in which married men can easily order up their fill of gay sex—discreetly, without having to go to a bar or some cruisey restroom—as if they're calling a Chinese place for takeout. They don't have to take risks, and can lead a secret life even more seamlessly. If we're going to traffic in clichés, maybe "throwback" isn't the one. Maybe we should be saying, the more things change, the more they stay the same.

New York Press, **May 25, 2004**

DON'T BLAME THE GAYS

A FEW WEEKS AGO Howard Dean told me that, oddly, I was the only interviewer to ask him about a passage in his new book, *You Have the Power,* in which he recounts how Bill Clinton told one of Dean's supporters that Dean "had forfeited his right to run for president." The reason for Clinton's alleged claim? Because Dean had signed civil unions into law in Vermont, something Clinton believed would prevent him from ever getting elected. The fact that few in the media asked Dean about this glaring account in his book—in a year in which one presidential candidate has used the issue of same-sex marriage against the other one—says a lot about our clueless media, which is suddenly telling us that the presidential election turned on "moral values."

It also obviously says a lot about Bill Clinton, though not much we didn't know already. The gay issue has always been complicated for Clinton, traumatized as he was on the gays-in-the-military issue and often operating from then on in an irrational manner. *Newsweek* claimed last week that Clinton had advised John Kerry during the campaign that he should come out in support of the various antigay state-ballot initiatives banning same-sex marriage, to which Kerry supposedly replied, "I'm not going to ever do that."

Kerry not only did the honorable thing, he was smart not to take the advice. That strategy would not have worked for the Democrats, not in 2004, and Kerry's loss might have been greater had he followed it, perhaps dampening turnout among a substantial part of his base. (Clinton, by the way, saw a dramatic drop in turnout among the 4 million or so gay voters in 1996 after he signed the Defense of Marriage Act and did not gain any conservative "values" voters—who gave more of their vote to Bob Dole that year than they did to George W. Bush in 2000—and Clinton never won with a majority of the electorate; he snagged a few red states mostly because Ross Perot ate into the Republican candidate's base a bit. Let's not forget that Al Gore, who supported more progay initiatives than Clinton, including partnership rights, won the majority of the popular vote in 2000.)

The entire "moral values" story of the 2004 election has been greatly exaggerated by the corporate media. Not so coincidentally, it fits exactly with what the Republicans would like everyone to believe. They'd like the Democrats to erupt into a civil war and would be thrilled to see the Democrats act on an impulse to now move to the right. And certainly the Republicans would like to perpetuate the image of Karl Rove as "boy genius," though Bush won reelection by the smallest margin of any incumbent since Woodrow Wilson and of any wartime president in history.

Dick Meyer at CBSNews.com notes that the exit polls that claim "moral values" trumped every other issue—from taxes to terrorism—were vague and exceedingly misleading. People were given a list of items to check off, with "moral values" on the list but not exactly defined. Anything could be considered "moral values," including Bush's attitude toward Osama bin Laden ("evil"). And if the other issues on the list were less specifically broken down, they might have topped "moral values."

"If, for example, one of the issues on the list was a combined 'terrorism and Iraq' [instead of each listed separately], it would have been the top concern of 34 percent of the electorate and nobody would be talking about moral values," Meyer observes. "If 'taxes, jobs and the economy' was on the list as one item instead of two, it would have been the topper at 25 percent. If, say, abortion rights, gay marriage and moral values were both on the list separately, the numbers would be very different."

That could be why, throughout the entire year, same-sex marriage was listed at the bottom of the list of issues important to the election, in just about every poll among all kinds of voters.

That's not to say that gay-bashing from the Republicans was not at an all-time high. In Kentucky, Senator Jim Bunning won reelection—even though he seems to be suffering from dementia—by having his surrogates call his opponent "limp-wristed." Right-wing Republican extremist Tom Coburn warned of "rampant lesbianism" in high schools and won a Senate race in Oklahoma. Jim DeMint said that gays should not be given jobs teaching in the schools and took a Senate seat in South Carolina.

Similarly, the Bush campaign and the Republican National Committee used fear, hatred, and religious dogmatism shamelessly against John Kerry, whose campaign rarely if ever responded. While Karl Rove energized Christian-right groups to get out the vote, using same-sex marriage and a whole host of issues—and using the Republican National Committee and its front groups to send out mailings and conduct telephone push polls that claimed that Kerry supported same-sex marriage—the Democratic Party worked to keep the issue quiet. They ducked and ran for cover. But as a certain cowboy says, you can run but you can't hide.

Rather than distancing themselves from San Francisco's Mayor Gavin Newsom, for example, Democrats should have lauded him for taking a moral stand, however much they may disagree on civil unions or same-sex marriage. Bill Clinton may not have supported same-sex marriage, but he did support gay rights and was vocal about it during his 1992 campaign. He garnered more of the gay vote than the more circumspect Al Gore and John Kerry—more than 75 percent—and certainly got the support of many others among the base who saw supporting civil rights as a priority. Taking a page out of the Republican playbook, Democrats should have sent out equally targeted and hard-hitting mailings focused on the Republican Party's attempt to change the Constitution of the United States and turn a minority group into second-class citizens, hitting the issue head-on rather than running from it.

That said, the "moral values" exit-poll story was overblown. What got lost is the fact that the vast majority of people polled—62 percent—support giving legal sanction to gay relationships (same-sex marriage or civil unions), including many in the red states. Even in states in which the antigay ballot measures passed, the margins by which people voted against them were much greater than they'd have been only a few years ago, including in Michigan, where 41 percent voted against the measure. In Ohio, a lot of people turned out to vote for president but didn't vote on the initiative, which lends credence to the argument that the amendments didn't necessarily draw out voters in great numbers.

There are a lot of issues the Democrats are going to have to examine before 2008. But scapegoating gays, Gavin Newsom, and the Massachusetts Supreme Court is just too easy. Not to mention that it's playing right into the Republicans' hands.

New York Press, **November 9, 2004**

BELTWAY BACKTRACK

AT FIRST THOUGHT, IT'S difficult to understand how the Human Rights Campaign, the Washington, D.C.–based gay group that employs slick and high-powered lobbyists, could stumble into the P.R. disaster it did in recent weeks. It becomes plausible only when you remind yourself that those who live on Planet Beltway often don't have a clue about what's happening back on Earth.

Soon after John Kerry's defeat, news leaked and spread via the gay blogs that HRC was axing its executive director, Cheryl Jacques, the former state senator who hailed from the bluest of the blue states and had been at HRC for less than a year. The group's board was sending her packing back to Massachusetts; the reasons cited were Jacques's supposed stridency—signing off on bumper stickers that said, "George Bush, You're Fired!"—and her postelection refusal to bend on the issue of marriage rights.

HRC officials, caught off guard as the group's board was convening in Las Vegas, confirmed the reports of Jacques's forced resignation and then went into damage-control mode, claiming that the firing was about Jacques' "management style." They adamantly denied that it had anything to do with marriage equality.

But a week later, HRC's heterosexual board cochair Michael Berman was quoted in a front-page story in the *New York Times* explaining why gays need to tone it down in order to reach out to red-state America. Berman, who will take a leadership role until a new executive director is found, went on to say that the group would be willing to back George W. Bush's radical plan to privatize Social Security if it meant gays and lesbians and their partners could be included under the benefit. This was like throwing gasoline on a fire, sending activists across the country into fits of anger.

Far be it from me to criticize someone for their sexuality— some of my best friends are straight—but when you're firing your lesbian executive director and telling the world you're going to moderate your positions—on the front page of the *New York Times,* no less—it's perhaps not the best time to make a straight guy the mouthpiece of your organization. Imagine if a man popped up as a spokesperson for the National Organization for Women, telling the press that NOW will be "moderating" a bit on the issue of abortion. What if a white guy took over as NAACP honcho to explain why the group should consider "compromising" on affirmative action in light of Bush's victory? Because of the endurance of the closet, gays are invisible enough in American culture and politics. When we have an opportunity to show the world what gay people actually look like—as when the leaders of our organizations speak to the press—we should take full advantage by actually having a gay person out front.

Berman's sexual orientation isn't even half the problem. Being quoted on the front page of the *Times* in support of controversial right-wing policies invites every other gay leader to knock you off your perch. That's what many did, as when the National Gay and Lesbian Task Force fired off a letter to every member of Congress, now signed by over 1,000 gay-rights activists.

"We specifically reject any attempts to trade equal rights for lesbian, gay, bisexual and transgender people, a group that includes many elders, for the rights of senior citizens under Social Security or, for that matter, the rights of any other group of Americans," the letter stated, initially signed by dozens of prominent gay-rights leaders.

It was a way of saying, "Don't mind that man behind the curtain" about HRC, a group that had convinced itself and many Beltway politicians that it was the Great and Powerful Oz of the gay-rights movement. And it could prove to be devastating. If you're a lobbying group, you need to let the Beltway believe you have either money or bodies—masses of voters to organize across the country who will follow your lead—or both. HRC, with a $25 million budget, is minuscule compared to the gun lobby or pro-Israel groups in terms of influence. If HRC can't convince politicians that its endorsement can deliver the gay vote—or that it even speaks for the gay-rights movement—what use is it?

Clearly thrown by the bold step of other activists—which the *Washington Post* focused on prominently the next day—HRC quickly tried to moderate its position on moderation. The group sent a letter to the *Times* insisting that the story wasn't accurate, and told anyone who inquired that they had not changed their commitment to full and equal rights under the law. However, the group refused to sign on to the letter to members of Congress, which served to support the worst charges about the group's initial intentions.

Soon Jacques's friends and colleagues were telling the *Boston Globe* that HRC had indeed fired her because she refused to back down on marriage. One of her defenders is the former Massachusetts attorney general, Scott Harshbarger, who is also a former president and CEO of Common Cause in Washington. In an interview, he said that to those outside the Beltway, HRC's approach looks naïve and self-defeating.

"But inside the Beltway," he told me, "this is the entire problem. This is the problem that John McCain exposed four years ago when he ran for president to the shock and surprise of so many people inside the Beltway. It's why the Democrats were shocked by Howard Dean, because there is an inside-the-Beltway mentality [that premises everything] in terms of being incremental, being so pragmatic and compromis[ing], as opposed to being willing to confront issues and try to deal with them head-on. You might lose, but at least you make a case and fight them another day."

HRC, Harshbarger added, has "undercut a lot of people" who supported gay rights.

"How'd you like to be a supporter of this issue [in Congress] who went out on a limb in a district where maybe it wasn't popular, and now find out that the leading advocacy organization is backing away from it?" he asked rhetorically. "It represents a weakness and a lack of courage."

It also represents a group that is out of touch with the gay-rights movement.

New York Press, **December 23, 2004**

INAUGURAL GALL

IT WAS BAD ENOUGH to learn that 23 percent of gay voters were delusional and self-loathing enough to again vote for George W. Bush, a man who has vowed to make them permanent second-class citizens by tinkering with the Constitution. Perhaps it wasn't all that surprising, since we all know that many of the boys in the Log Cabin Republicans love bending over and taking it long and hard, and seem to have quite a high threshold for abuse. Still, even the Log Cabin leadership—which withheld an endorsement of Bush—must have been thrown by that figure, since it evaporated any bit of bargaining power gay Republicans might have had. Log Cabin ran ads against Bush, spoke out against the federal marriage amendment, and even (lightly) defended John Kerry's much-criticized mention of Mary Cheney's lesbianism during the debate. (Actually, they said Kerry should have kept his mouth shut, but that Dick Cheney and the Republicans were hypocrites to suddenly start criticizing others as insensitive to gays and lesbians.)

Perhaps the Log Cabinites' most memorable and devastating move was to threaten Republicans by noting that if Bush backed the FMA, he risked losing those one million gay voters—25 percent of the total gay vote—who voted for him in 2000 but might not turn out in 2004 without a Log Cabin endorsement.

Yet, even after the FMA, the "moral values" campaign and an unprecedented GOP gay-bashing campaign—and after Log Cabin withheld an endorsement—the exact same number of gay voters (according to the exit polls) cast a vote for Bush, proving that Log Cabin has little influence on anyone.

If it was hideous to learn that so many gay voters supported Bush, finding out that the head of a major gay-founded AIDS advocacy group in Washington is on the Inaugural Committee—thus lending the cause of AIDS activism to Bush's celebration—is completely incomprehensible. It's particularly galling considering the flat-funding of domestic AIDS dollars we've seen come from the Bush administration, as well as the administration's murderous promotion of bogus abstinence-only programs for American teenagers at the expense of condom-education programs. In December, a report released by Representative Henry Waxman revealed that some abstinence-only programs told kids that HIV could be spread via sweat and tears, and that half of all gay teens were infected—a complete fabrication and a recipe for gay-bashing in our schools.

It's mind-boggling that anyone who considered themselves a

leader on AIDS would associate their group and cause with so callous a president. But that appears to be the case with AIDS Action's Marsha Martin. On his blog, Direland.com, veteran political journalist Doug Ireland blew the whistle over the holidays on Martin, head of AIDS Action, which bills itself as the "voice of action" and claims to lead thousands of AIDS groups as the most powerful AIDS lobby in Washington.

Martin, Ireland writes, has "jumped into bed with the Bush-Rove Republicans with both feet," putting her name on an inaugural celebration that will benefit the deceptively named AIDS Responsibility Project. The ARP is a group that fights the approval and use of generic drugs to treat HIV in poorer nations, allowing Bush's buddies in Big Pharma to make a literal killing on AIDS. ARP, according to Advocate.com, took out a full-page ad in the *Bangkok Post,* attacking the use of generic drugs by inaccurately claiming they're ineffective. The Center for Media and Democracy describes the ARP as a pharmaceutical industry front group that boasts a "partnership" with the Pharmaceutical Research and Manufacturers of America (PhRMA).

"Salute a Second Term: Celebrating Freedom, Honoring Service: An Inaugural Dinner Invitation," is how the invitation listing Martin's name reads. "You are cordially invited to join in celebrating the Presidential Inauguration and Republican electoral success."

That people like Martin are so easily bought—selling their souls in return for participating in what is being billed as the most expensive inauguration in history—underscores how Bush co-opted much of the AIDS movement under his "compassionate conservative" banner, making it appear as if he's done a great deal to combat the epidemic when in fact he's made it worse. Meanwhile, he's got his supporters running the Big

Pharma front groups, posing as AIDS activists. ARP is run by Abner Mason, a Log Cabin Republican and Bush supporter who did little to advance the cause against AIDS when he sat on the Presidential AIDS Commission. That panel—created by Bill Clinton and critical of the president's efforts during the Clinton years—has given Bush a rubber stamp since Day One. That's because Bush reconfigured the panel and installed all of his own backers—as he is now doing with the Civil Rights Commission—including many abstinence-only devotees. For a while it was led by Tom Coburn, the viciously antigay former Republican House member who was just elected to the U.S. Senate in Oklahoma after warning the electorate of rampant lesbianism in the state's schools.

Bush and Karl Rove are masters when it comes to playing people, but you do have to be a pretty craven fool yourself to be taken in. Since election day, we've heard the rumbling of moderation and acquiescence to Bush from the Human Rights Campaign—though they have staunchly denied it—when the nation's largest gay lobby was reported in the *New York Times* as being more willing to bend to red-state America and might even accept Bush's draconian privatization plan for Social Security. Now we have the leader of the nation's largest AIDS lobby helping to toast the new president and asking others to join her in plunking down money—$125 to $5,000—to benefit a group that will help Bush's friends in the drug industry and hurt people with AIDS around the world. We're losing the battle not because the religious right is so powerful—most Americans staunchly disagree with them—but because our own leaders are so weak.

New York Press, **January 4, 2005**

$5,000 AN IDEA, FULL-SERVICE

"**WELL, OKAY, STOP FOR** just a second," CNN's Carol Costello told Maggie Gallagher, one of three (so far) conservative columnists exposed in recent weeks for taking cash from the Bush administration in exchange for promoting its policies. "Stop—let me get a word in edgewise here."

Gallagher, a grimacing little tyrant with jet black hair and a round pink face, was in foot-stomping mode, angry that anyone would dare compare her to Armstrong Williams, the Tribune Media Services columnist who took money from the Department of Education in return for talking up Bush education policy in his column and media appearances. But the similarities between the two are striking. Both are no-talent vipers who prostitute themselves as members of groups (blacks and women) into which conservatives would love to drive a wedge. Both also babble incoherently with little grasp of facts.

In a November 18, 2004, column offering advice to Democrats in the aftermath of the election, Williams wrote that Bill Clinton "was waddling all over [Washington] in the months leading up to the election, imploring [Democratic] party leaders to abandon their support of a gay marriage amendment."

Gay marriage amendment? Democrats? There was of course the Federal Marriage Amendment, pushed by conservative Republicans and George W. Bush, to ban gays from marrying, writing their second-class citizenship into the Constitution. But there was no shadow "gay marriage amendment" attempting to legalize same-sex marriage. This is a complete delusion on the part of Williams—one that his editors at Tribune Media for some reason allowed to be published.

"Despite the rhetoric you hear from the homosexual Cosa Nostra, the lack of support for the gay marriage amendment has nothing to do with prejudice . . . ," he continued, in his alternate universe. "Somehow, though, the Democrats don't get this. They hang on to the gay marriage amendment with mind-numbing intransigence."

It comes as no surprise that someone so out of touch with reality should also be mired in self-denial. Williams, like Gallagher, uses the "homosexual agenda" as a whipping post, and in his case the irony is deep, indeed. Williams has been accused of male-on-male sexual harassment (the case was settled out of court) and David Brock claims in *Blinded by the Right* that Williams once made a pass at him in Williams's apartment, allegedly asking Brock if he was "dominant or submissive in bed."

I brought up the alleged Brock pass to Williams at the Republican National Convention in August, where he was busy cavorting about with Tina Brown, whose equally incoherent talk show he'd appeared on several times last year. In response to my question about rumors that he is another self-loathing, right-wing closet case, Williams babbled nervously for a while before denying he was gay. He then thanked me for being "so kind to ask me these questions," noting that, "I've been through the fire and I'm still standing."

Gallagher is prone to similar nonsensical emissions, but heatedly denies the payola charge. She didn't take money for promoting Bush's marriage initiative in the media, she explained on CNN. Rather, like the most recently exposed columnist on the take, "Ethics and Religion" syndicated columnist Michael McManus, Gallagher was merely paid by the Department of Health and Human Services to write official materials. In other words, Gallagher and McManus were paid to *actually write* the government's propaganda, while Williams was paid to *propagandize* the government's propaganda. There is a difference, you see.

In fact, Gallagher's crime is far more egregious than Williams's, despite the latter having made $240,000 for his efforts, while Gallagher made off with only a little over $40,000 ($21,500 for writing the government's marriage-initiative brochures, and a subsequent payment of $20,000). What few media reports noted last week was that Gallagher, in addition to writing the Bush administration brochures and pumping up its policies in her columns, testified before a Senate subcommittee in support of the Federal Marriage Amendment that the White House eventually backed and pushed throughout the presidential campaign. But Gallagher was not identified before the Senate Committee on the Judiciary and Subcommittee on the Constitution, Civil Rights and Property Rights as the individual who wrote the White House's policy on marriage, but rather as the president of the Institute for Marriage and Public Policy, an independent think tank. She was thus a paid witness on behalf of the Bush administration, testifying before the Senate.

Moreover, Gallagher's stature as an "expert" before the committee was enhanced by her stint as an anonymous writer of Bush's policy a year earlier—a spectacular example of sleazy self-promotion. On his blog Soundbitten.com, Greg Beato explains how Gallagher actually promoted her own book by ghostwriting for the government:

> In return for the $21,500, Gallagher's primary task was to draft a 3000-word essay for one Wade Horn, assistant secretary for children and families in the U.S. Department of Health and Human Services. Ultimately, the essay was published by *Crisis* magazine; in it, Gallagher, writing as Horn, exclaims: "Adults, too, benefit from healthy and stable marriages. They tend to live longer, healthier lives and are more affluent. Married mothers suffer from considerably lower rates of depression than their single counterparts. Like a good education, a good marriage is a real asset. Married men earn between 10 and 40 percent more than similar single men, and married couples accumulate substantially more wealth. By the time they're ready to retire, married couples have, on average, assets worth two and a half times as much as their single counterparts." (The figure for married couples is $410,000, compared with $167,000 for those who never married and $154,000 for divorced individuals, according to Linda J. Waite and Maggie Gallagher in their book, *The Case for Marriage*.)

The day before Gallagher testified before the Senate sub-committee, she appeared on my radio program to argue her—and the Bush administration's—case. She quickly devolved into advocating some rather bizarre ideas, such as that gay people, in order to gain marriage rights, marry heterosexuals and have children, while remaining gay and sexually active.

"I think it's a very a high-risk thing to do, and I don't recommend it," she said. "But I'm not barring the door. I think mixed marriages are fine."

Gallagher would rather have people live a lie for the sake of the "children" than have them be open, honest and self-accepting—the healthiest environment for both children and parents. Is it any wonder that deceit and nondisclosure are Maggie Gallagher's stock-in-trade?

New York Press, **February 1, 2005**

CALLING OUT GUCKERT

WHEN IT RAINS EXPOSED hacks, it sure pours exposed hacks! First there was Armstrong Williams, the dimwit who took money from the Bush administration to push its education policies on television and in his columns. Then there was Maggie Gallagher, the onetime single mom who believes everyone should be made to marry—except for gays, who should be prevented from doing so through a constitutional amendment—and who was paid to write administration policy on the subject for government brochures while hawking herself as an independent pundit. Gallagher was followed by Michael McManus, an "Ethics and Religion" columnist who certainly wasn't being ethical when he took money from the Bush administration, though he did it religiously.

The latest "journalist" with a curious relationship to the White House is James Guckert, aka Jeff Gannon, who wrote antigay screeds and gay-baited John Kerry—possibly the first "gay president," he said in one of his leading questions during press conference—but who now looks to have been associated with gay-hustler-themed Web sites while mysteriously gaining access to daily White House briefings.

To listen to the arrogant and suddenly pious anchors and reporters of the corporate press corps—who've hardly been guardians of privacy in recent years—it's all just so unseemly. The hand-wringing over liberal bloggers' supposed revelations about the fake White House reporter's "personal life" has been comical; and no matter what they say, it certainly does not reflect any newfound regard for privacy. It looks more like the media got beat, again, on a story that was sitting right under their noses. Playing catch-up, they had to create a backstory that also acted as an alibi. Thus all the talk about the brutality of the bloggers who beat them to the punch.

Like bratty kids made to eat their greens, CNN, the *Washington Post, New York Times,* and other news organizations were eventually forced to report on how a fraud using a false name and working for a right-wing Web site owned by a Republican Party operative in Texas—Talon News—gained access to daily White House press briefings for two years. Guckert even appears to have seen or known about (he declined to tell *Editor & Publisher* when asked) a memo that outed Valerie Plame, Ambassador Joe Wilson's wife, as an undercover CIA agent.

Guckert's escapades came to light only because liberal Web sites and blogs shined a bright light on him and began investigating his background. David Brock's site, Media Matters for America (MediaMatters.org), pointed to the guy's habit of plagiarizing material from Republican press releases. *Daily Kos* and

Atrios were also on the case, looking into his phony name, his background and how he was often called upon by spokesman Scott McClellan, seemingly to deflect attention. At first, the corporate press was silent. This possibly served to embolden Gannon, who actually dared the bloggers to come and get him, writing on his own Web site, JeffGannon.com, that he was "hiding in plain sight."

But soon thereafter the blogs revealed that a company Gannon owned also ran Web sites with military gay-hustler themes, including hotmilitarystud.com and militaryescortsm4m.com and others. A photo of Guckert in his America Online profile also surfaced, showing him in only his briefs and military dog tags, suggestively positioned in a "let's fuck" pose, above the caption, "Still sexy after all these years." Within hours, Guckert announced on his Web site that his "voice" was now "silent," and that he had resigned from Talon News. Talon then scrubbed their site of anything to do with the guy. That's when the corporate press was forced to cover this story, choosing to portray it as one in which liberal bloggers—as opposed to the "responsible" media—went overboard.

On CNN, the *Washington Post*'s Howard Kurtz asked Wolf Blitzer if these "liberal bloggers" went "too far . . . in dragging in some of this personal stuff."

Of course, Kurtz thought the answer was a resounding yes, even though the Web sites suggested a connection to the prostitution of military personnel, something Kurtz failed to mention. On CNN's *Newsnight,* Aaron Brown, who often romanticizes the "craft" of journalism, seemed to be grasping for ways to excuse his and other news organizations for not reporting on a guy who had been in their midst for two years. The first question he asked John Aravosis of Americablog, which was at the forefront of exposing Gannon, was: "There is,

I think here, a kind of 'so-what' quality. Here's this guy, everyone knows what he is, the only people honestly who read the Web site are people who believe what he believes to begin with. So why the fuss?"

Brown also floated the White House line that White House staffers don't decide who gets into the White House briefings, to which Aravosis simply replied, "That is the biggest bunch of hogwash I've ever heard." We know how much this White House controls press briefing and who asks questions. Brown also lamented, "[there's] something a little unseemly about the way . . . people went after this guy's personal life." Aravosis cut through that one, too, noting that the Web sites—which Guckert himself told CNN were sites he created for clients when he was trying to launch a software company—were about his "business" life, not his "personal" life, and showed a connection to escort services. Brown seemed not to want to go near the Plame angle at all—which gives major legitimacy to the story—deciding to end it right there in hopes the story just goes away.

The story, like many, may, in fact, go away. Or, if Democrats continue to call for investigations (Senator Frank Lautenberg demanded records from McClellan, while two Democratic House members demanded that the special prosecutor on the Plame case investigate Guckert), it may have legs. But why, in addition to the general free ride the media has given Bush on a host of issues, was the press corps so reluctant to go after this story? Because they didn't want to upset the applecart—that is, the White House press-briefing room.

Just like the Pentagon press-briefing room, White House reporters are fed little morsels of information. Anybody who causes trouble—by exposing, say, a White House plant in the room—is going to get punished, and thus be denied access and get scooped by the competition. As a result, someone like Gannon operated among them for two years without being exposed, even though they all knew—and were clearly embarrassed by—the truth.

New York Press, **February 16, 2005**

LOG CABIN'S DRUG MONEY

AFTER ALL THE HOMOPHOBIA that spewed during campaign 2004, the Log Cabin Republicans amazingly continue to grovel before the Bush White House, even as Karl Rove has decided they're not even worth licking the dirt from under his toenails. A lot of people thought that Log Cabin's refusal to endorse George W. Bush during the election campaign was some sort of turning point for the group. I remember running into a gay Democratic fund-raiser at the Log Cabin's "Big Tent" event during the Republican National Convention, at the Bryant Park Grill in Manhattan.

"This is a new Log Cabin," he told me. "This is a big deal that they are not going to endorse him. Finally we're seeing the group having matured and realizing that it can't just be used. That's why I've helped them raise money and am supporting them, even though I'm a Democrat."

I rolled my eyes, knowing that any spine on the part of Log Cabin was a mere aberration. And here we are, just a few months after Rove and Bush used the Federal Marriage Amendment to gay-bash their way to reelection, and the Log Cabinites have announced they're offering to help Bush push through his draconian Social Security privatization plan—perhaps because they're quietly on the dole from the multinational corporations that would benefit under the plan. The Bushies are so desperate to light a fire under their dud of a "reform" plan—with Bush on a sixty-day, sixty-stop tour—you'd think they'd take all the help they can get. But so far, the only use they've had for gays in this effort has been to once again make them into Willie Hortons, using images of gay men to smear groups that oppose Bush. And that underscores how absolutely devoid of integrity and starved for validation the Log Cabinites really are.

Last month, in the same week in which the Republican front group USA Next ran ads using a gay Oregon couple to tar the American Association for Retired Persons (AARP) because it didn't support Bush's plan, the Log Cabinites told ABC News they were going to aid Bush in breathing life into his dead-on-arrival privatization plan.

"Now the election of 2004 is over," Christopher Barron, the Log Cabin Republicans' political director told ABC. "And we think there are opportunities to work with this president. The fact is the gay and lesbian community has to realize that the president won."

His timing couldn't have been worse. Just as Barron was making those comments, USA Next, which includes some of the Swift Boat Veterans assassins who slimed John Kerry, began running the now-infamous ads showing the Oregon men in tuxedos kissing just after they were married, above the tag line, "The Real AARP Agenda." The idea, of course, was to demonize the AARP, which has been vocal against Bush's plan. Charlie Jarvis, the head of USA Next, told the *New York Times* that the AARP is a "boulder" in the "middle of the highway" to Social Security privatization, and that his group was the "dynamite" that would remove it by spending $10 million on ads showing AARP to be a radical "liberal" organization.

Like the rest of the right-wing hatchet men, Jarvis isn't above deceit and trickery, as AARP—a nearly fifty-year-old nonpartisan group that has lobbied on behalf of senior citizens and actually sided with Bush on his appallingly duplicitous prescription drug bill in late 2003—had no position on same-sex marriage. Even as the gay couple has now launched a $25 million lawsuit against USA Next for using their image—and a federal judge last week issued a temporary restraining order against the group—the White House has refused to condemn the ads.

The fact that a gay Republican group would actually pledge to help the White House in its quest to privatize Social Security even as the White House's front group is using gays as a whipping post on the issue is outrageous. And many gay Republicans around the country—many of them current and former Log Cabin members—are decrying this ugly pandering. One member from Oregon wrote me last week to say it had forced him to make the step and register as a Democrat.

But Log Cabin's leadership perhaps has no choice if it wants to see its money sources left intact, as it is bankrolled by an industry that is heavily backing Bush and his privatization plan. For years now it has been evident that Log Cabin couldn't possibly exist on its measly membership and its dues. For a long time the group has taken money from pharmaceutical companies such a Glaxo-Wellcome and Pfizer—in $50,000 to $150,000 contributions. Log Cabin has in return acted as a lobbying arm for Big Pharma, urging Congress not to allow generic AIDS drugs in foreign countries, for example, even at the cost of millions of lives around the world. Having gays lobby against cheaper AIDS drugs has a certain cachet—like having blacks lobby against affirmative action—and in that way Log Cabin can be of value to the right.

It has also helped some Log Cabin leaders to parlay their meager influence-peddling in bigger jobs as full-out drug industry shills. Abner Mason, a onetime national president of Log Cabin Republicans and a member of Bush's presidential AIDS commission, now heads the curiously titled AIDS Responsibility Project (ARP), a front group for the drug industry that lobbies to stop generic drugs. (That someone shilling for the pharmaceutical industry is on Bush's AIDS commission also points to the fact that the commission, under Bush, is a complete travesty.) Rich Tafel, former executive director of Log Cabin, is on the ARP board and has his own company, RLT Strategies, which has also lobbied foreign governments and corporations on behalf of American drug companies.

Ironically, the same drug companies fund USA Next, the group that is using homophobia to bash the AARP. Under a different name (United Seniors Association), USA Next shilled for the pharmaceutical companies during the congressional battle over the prescription drug bill in 2003. The Pharmaceutical Research and Manufacturers of America funded most of a $4.6 million ad campaign launched that year by USA targeting both Democrats and Republicans who opposed the deceptive prescription bill, which Bush ultimately pushed through in part by lying about the price tag. The drug companies of course don't care who gets hurt by privatizing Social Security. Their only concern is making more profit, even if that means funding groups that bash gays to achieve their agenda, or giving money to those gay people who are so greedy and lacking in dignity that they'll help out in the bashing.

Signorile.com, March 15, 2005

GAY ABE AND SAPPHIC SUSAN

HAVING MYSELF OUTED A dead man—the publishing tycoon Malcolm Forbes—back in the spring of 1990 (while some of his sanitized obituaries were still being written), I've curiously watched the uneven coverage of Susan Sontag's life and death in recent weeks, as well as the critics' treatments of the late Kinsey researcher C. A. Tripp's controversial book, *The Intimate World of Abraham Lincoln*.

Outing the dead still isn't easy. There is a conspiracy of silence pervading the living, particularly in the journalistic and intellectual class. While the Tripp book has received some positive reviews, the negative ones have been much more telling. These generally take two forms.

Some portray Tripp, who died at eighty-six, as having been off his rocker, his book filled with quaint Kinseyeque psychobabble and clichés. His arguments, they claim, are all speculative—such as when he obsesses about Lincoln's use of the words "yours forever" in his letters to Joshua Speed.

Others argue that the evidence might be there—Lincoln and Speed did share a tiny bed with one another each night for four years, which even by Frontier America standards seems a bit queer—but even if it is true, why does it matter now?

In the case of Sontag, the excuses for the sloppy coverage have been less pointed, but no less obscuring. The *New York Times* and *Los Angeles Times* omitted any reference to the influential writer's sapphic romances, while *People* and CNN mentioned that she had been involved with the photographer Annie Leibovitz. The crawl on WABC-TV actually called Leibovitz Sontag's "longtime companion," while the gay press spoke more fully about Sontag's relationships with other women, including Lucinda Childs. In response to a slew of letters—including a few from longtime activist Ann Northrop, which have made the rounds—the *Times*'s public editor, Daniel Okrent, sent out a response claiming that the *Times* couldn't verify Sontag's sexuality with Sontag's son, David Reiff—who would neither confirm nor deny—and that Leibovitz would not comment, either. Okrent's response was sent out only via e-mail, and has yet to actually make it into the paper.

Okrent's defense presupposes that the *Times* never prints anything about public figures' sexual lives unless the individuals involved or their survivors verify the facts. Of course, there are countless examples of the *Times* printing accounts regarding the sexual lives of heterosexual public figures, living and dead, without confirmation from the subjects and their partners. But in the case of Malcolm Forbes, another nonheterosexual public figure, the *Times* did so—albeit a few years after the fact.

Shortly after Forbes died, I wrote a cover story for *OutWeek* magazine, which included accounts from both named and unnamed sources attesting to Forbes's having engaged in sex with men, most of them individuals who'd worked at *Forbes* magazine. Some of these people were men who'd actually had sex with Forbes.

It's quite laughable looking back on it now, but no one wanted to touch the story. New York's *Daily News* had heard about it a week before, and negotiated an exclusive with *Out-Week,* with plans to put it on their cover the day the magazine hit the stands. But they got cold feet at the last minute, and instead ran with the suitably heterosexual scandal and headline: "Marla Hid in Trump Tower."

It took weeks for the Forbes story to trickle out, mostly in articles about the supposedly new practice of "outing," which was described as despicable. Some papers still wouldn't mention the dead Forbes by name. In its story, the *Times* would refer only to a "recently deceased businessman" who'd been outed. The *Times* clearly saw outing the dead as distasteful, and, as with Sontag, editors certainly weren't going to dig deep enough to verify homosexuality.

Six years later, however, in an article about Malcolm's son Steve Forbes, the *Times* discussed "the first published reports in the gay press of his father's homosexuality," and even gave us this sensational little tidbit, which appeared to have been lifted from my *OutWeek* story: "In the last few years of his life Malcolm Forbes became increasingly indiscreet, and he was seen roaring up on his motorcycle in tight black leather to Manhattan nightclubs, and, according to current and former workers at [*Forbes*] magazine, pursuing some of his young male employees."

The *Times* had no independent verification; editors had

simply been emboldened by the passage of time. In the case of Sontag, the hypocrisy is even greater, since she had acknowledged affairs with other women herself—in *The New Yorker* and in an interview in *Out* magazine—even if she was circumspect about her sexual identity and her relationship with Leibovitz.

Likewise, it is not as if C. A. Tripp is delving into a subject that hasn't been discussed before. Going back to the 1920s, historians have hinted at the possibility that Abe Lincoln had a male lover. In his *Salon* review, however, Andrew O'Hehir rather harshly accuses Gore Vidal and Doug Ireland of being "apologists" for Tripp, saying the evidence just isn't solid enough to herald the book, as both Vidal and Ireland have done. But when outing the dead—particularly someone as long dead as Lincoln—it's not the one smoking gun that is going to make the case, but rather the cumulative effect of circumstantial evidence.

To those who like to point to Lincoln's having been married and had children, I would point to Forbes and Sontag having done the same. And Tripp—like a few other historians—has shown that Lincoln's sexual life with the women he courted and married was not exactly on fire. Using his experience and knowledge as a Kinsey sex researcher—this methodology does admittedly get a bit loopy, fascinating as it may sometimes be— Tripp discusses several men who could have been Lincoln's male lovers and at least one, Speed, who most probably was. Writing a review in the *New York Times,* Richard Brookhiser, the conservative *New York Observer* writer, seems willing to accept that, but doesn't think it important.

"Tripp can lay out a case, but his discussion of its implications is so erratic that the reader is often left on his own," he writes. "One wonders: What does it mean to be homosexual?"

This dismissive question denies a century of the religious

right's growth and eventual dominance over Lincoln's Republican Party. It also ignores the party's current demonizing of those who engage in sex with people of the same sex while sanctifying heterosexual marriage and the family. Of course Lincoln wasn't "gay" in the sense of the word today, as the categories of sexual identity didn't exist in his lifetime. But if every school kid learned that Honest Abe, in addition to having married Mary Todd, also had some very intimate male buddies, he or she might think a lot differently about what "gay" is now.

New York Press, **January 18, 2005**

ACKNOWLEDGMENTS

THIS COLLECTION WOULD NOT be possible without many editors, from various publications, with whom I worked over the years. I'm especially grateful to Judy Gerber, Michael Goff, Elise Harris, Paul Schindler, Bruce Steele, Robin Stevens, and Judy Wieder.

As editor of *Out Magazine,* the late Sarah Pettit not only rigorously oversaw several of the pieces included here; she taught me a great deal about culture, politics, writing, and friendship in her painfully short life, something for which I'll always be thankful.

Many of the latter pieces in this collection evolved from— or were expanded upon on—my daily radio program on Sirius Satellite Radio. The show and the listeners who interact on a daily basis—as well as the broad array of guests, accomplished in every field imaginable—have become my passion and my inspiration. A big thank you goes to my hard-working producer, Anthony Veneziano.

Don Weise, my editor at Carroll and Graf, had a vision for this collection and saw it through, treating my work with care. I consider myself very fortunate to have worked with him.

My agent, Fred Morris, is a long-time friend and a wise advisor, always looking out for me. That was equally true of his mentor, the late Jed Mattes, whose influence on my early work was profound. Mitchell Ivers, who edited my three previous books, is a friend who is always there when I need him; he offered his input on many of the pieces here.

I'm thankful to the political junkie pals who help fuel my thoughts and ideas, including Drew Beaver, Doria Biddle, Joel Lawson, Gabriel Rotello, and Corey Johnson.

Similarly, many of the ideas in these pieces were inspired by bloggers whose work has helped keep me sane in these Bush years. In particular I'm grateful to Duncan Black at *Atrios* (www.atrios.blogspot.com); James Capozzola at *Rittenhouse Review* (www.rittenhouse.blogspot.com); all of the folks at DailyKos.com; John Byrne of Rawstory.com; Mike Rogers of Blogactive.com; and Americablog.com, which is run by the indefatigable web activist John Aravosis.

The ten years that this collection spans is also the same ten years in which I have been with my partner David Gerstner, whose love has kept me going and whose scholarly work challenges me and inspires me.

ABOUT THE AUTHOR

MICHELANGELO SIGNORILE hosts a daily talk show on Sirius Satellite Radio's OutQ. Signorile has been an editor-at-large and a columnist at *The Advocate*, and a columnist for *OUT* magazine, and has written for *The New York Times, USA Today, The New York Observer, New York Magazine*, and the *Village Voice*. He's appeared on *Larry King Live, Good Morning America, Today, 60 Minutes*, and other shows. He lives in New York City. He can be reached at www.signorile.com.